Yet with all their inglorious defects and weaknesses, it is the poor who emerge as the true heroes of contemporary Mexico, for they are paying the cost of the industrial progress of the nation. Indeed, the political stability of Mexico is grim testimony to the great capacity for misery and suffering of the ordinary Mexican.

Oscar Lewis,
The Children of Sanchez, 1961

juárez

the laboratory of our future

**APERTURE GRATEFULLY ACKNOWLEDGES THE
GENEROUS SUPPORT OF THE LANNAN FOUNDATION,
WHICH MADE THIS BOOK POSSIBLE.**

juárez
the laboratory of our future

CHARLES BOWDEN

PREFACE BY NOAM CHOMSKY

AFTERWORD BY EDUARDO GALEANO

PHOTOGRAPHS BY JAVIER AGUILAR, JAIME BAILLERES, GABRIEL CARDONA,
JULIÁN CARDONA, ALFREDO CARRILLO, RAÚL LODOZA, JAIME MURRIETA,
MIGUEL PEREA, MARGARITA REYES, ERNESTO RODRÍGUEZ,
MANUEL SÁENZ, LUCIO SORIA ESPINO, AURELIO SUÁREZ NÚÑEZ

APERTURE

. . . I found on the desk in my office one of your letters in which you told me of your visit to Vallejo and Campa [two leaders of the railroad workers union imprisoned since 1959 on the charge of promoting "social dissolution" under Article 143 of the Federal Penal Code]. What a shame and what a tragedy! One tends to forget the most painful things, surrounding one-self with a sort of vast silence that suddenly is broken by many sounds. That splendid, self-ish silence behind which we protect our egos and lose touch with our true selves. How is it possible for us to each live our own separate lives: so "comfortable," so well sheltered, so indifferent? It pains me greatly to imagine Vallejo, a tiny little figure in his cell that is as neat as a pin, drinking milk like a cat, hoping that some day he will be released and go back to . . . to what exactly? To a street somewhere and little knots of people who will stare at him with a certain curiosity, but also with a fundamental indifference. What is he going to do when he gets out? How is he going to live? Whom is he going to love? How is he going to work? This frightens me even more than the thought of him there in his cell drinking milk.

Guillermo Haro, astronomer, in a letter to Elena Poniatowska from Armenia, 22 July 1970

Now all the authorities
They just stand around and boast
How they blackmailed the sergeant-at-arms
Into leaving his post.

Bob Dylan, "Just Like Tom Thumb's Blues," 1965

. . . we will never be free, that's what I tell you, because we will be enslaved all our lives. Want to see it more clearly? Every government official that comes in, bites us, cripples us, leaves us maimed, toothless, lame and with our flesh and bones, builds his house.

Elena Poniatowska, *Hasta no verte Jesús mío*, 1969

All photographs taken from 1992 to 1997 in Ciudad Juárez, Chihuahua, México. Some of the images have been slightly cropped for reproduction in this book.

Pages 2–3: Jaime Bailleres. *An entrance to the Lote Bravo, an area of the desert surrounding Ciudad Juárez where dozens of the bodies of primarily Cd. Juárez citizens who have been raped and otherwise tortured and then murdered have been discovered since 1992.*

Pages 4–5: Jaime Bailleres. *Colonia Insurgentes, on the west side of Cd. Juárez. (In México,* colonia *refers to both new settlements, often shantytowns, and more established neighborhoods.) In the distance, downtown El Paso, Texas.*

Pages 6–7: Jaime Bailleres. *On the afternoon of 21 Septem-*

ber 1993, about 300 Mexicans protesting new U.S. Border Blockade Operation measures blocked the Puente Internacional Paso del Norte (also known as the Puente Santa Fe), one of the six bridges joining Cd. Juárez with El Paso. About 120 U.S. Border Patrol agents quickly arrived, armed with sticks to fight the Mexican demonstrators.

Pages 8–9: Jaime Bailleres. *Also on 21 September 1993, a* coyote *(a person who helps would-be illegal immigrants to cross the border) watches a* mojado *(pejoratively translated as "wetback") crossing the river, while U.S. Border Patrol agents continue to guard the Puente Internacional Paso del Norte.*

Above: Jaime Bailleres. *The body of a woman allegedly executed by* narcotraficantes *(drug traffickers) in Cd. Juárez.*

FOR RICHARD VONIER, REPORTER AND
EDITOR, AND PAUL DICKERSON, ARTIST.
THEY DIDN'T GO TO JUÁREZ BUT THEY'VE
SPENT A LOT OF TIME THERE WITH ME
ANYWAY. I'LL MISS THE PLEASURE OF
THEIR COMPANY AND THE EXCITEMENT
OF WATCHING THEIR GIFTS BRUSH UP
AGAINST THE WORLD.

—Charles Bowden

IN REMEMBRANCE OF ALL THE CHILDREN,
TEENAGERS, WOMEN, AND MEN WHO
HAVE BEEN VICTIMS OF THE VIOLENCE
AND POVERTY IN CIUDAD JUÁREZ.

—Javier Aguilar, Jaime Bailleres,
Gabriel Cardona, Julián Cardona,
Alfredo Carrillo, Raúl Lodoza,
Jaime Murrieta, Miguel Perea,
Margarita Reyes, Ernesto Rodríguez,
Manuel Sáenz, Lucio Soria Espino,
Aurelio Suárez Núñez, Carlos Vigueras

Notes On NAFTA

THE MASTERS OF MANKIND

NOAM CHOMSKY

Throughout history, Adam Smith observed, we find the workings of "the vile maxim of the masters of mankind": "All for ourselves, and nothing for other People." He had few illusions about the consequences. The invisible hand, he wrote, will destroy

the possibility of a decent human existence "unless government takes pains to prevent" this outcome, as must be assured in "every improved and civilized society." It will destroy community, the environment, and human values generally—and even the masters themselves, which is why the business classes have regularly called for state intervention to protect them from market forces.

The masters of mankind in Smith's day were the "merchants and manufacturers," who were the "principal architects" of state policy, using their power to bring "dreadful misfortunes" to the vast realms they subjugated and to harm the people of England as well, though their own interests were "most peculiarly attended to." In our day the masters are, increasingly, the supranational corporations and financial institutions that dominate the world economy, including international trade—a dubious term for a system in which some 40 percent of the U.S. trade takes place within companies, centrally managed by the same highly visible hands that control planning, production, and investment.

The World Bank reports that protectionist measures of the industrialized countries reduce national income in the South by about twice the amount of official aid to the region—aid that is itself largely

Ernesto Rodríguez. *Cardboard housing in Colonia Los Alcaldes, Cd. Juárez. There are about 400 colonias in the city. Homes are sometimes made from found materials, including waste from the* maquiladoras, *or* maquilas *(factories).*

export promotion, most of it directed to richer sectors (less needy, but better consumers). In the past decade, most of the rich countries have increased protectionism, with the Reaganites often leading the way in the crusade against economic liberalism. These practices, along with the programs dictated by the International Monetary Fund (IMF) and World Bank, have helped double the gap between rich and poor countries since 1960. Resource transfers from the poor to the rich amounted to more than $400 billion from 1982 to 1990, "the equivalent in today's dollars of some six Marshall Plans provided by the South to the North," observes Susan George of the Transnational Institute in Amsterdam; she notes also that commercial banks were protected by transfer of their bad debts to the public sector. As in the case of the S&Ls, and advanced industry generally, "free-market capitalism" is to be risk-free for the masters, as fully as can be achieved.

The international class war is reflected in the United States, where real wages have fallen to the level of the mid-1960s. Wage stagnation, extending to the college-educated, changed to sharp decline in the mid-1980s, in part a consequence of the decline in "defense spending," our euphemism for the state industrial policy that allows "private enterprise" to feed at the public trough. More than seventeen million workers were unemployed or underemployed by mid-1992, Economic Policy Institute economists Lawrence Mishel and Jared Bernstein report—a rise of eight million during the Bush years. Some 75 percent of that is permanent loss of jobs. Of the limited gain in total wealth in the eighties, "70 percent accrued to the top 1 percent of income earners, while the bottom lost absolutely," according to MIT economist Rudiger Dornbusch.

Structures of governance have tended to coalesce around economic power. The process continues. In the London *Financial Times*, James Morgan describes the "de facto world government" that is taking shape in the "new imperial age": the IMF, World Bank, Group of Seven industrialized nations, General Agreement on Tariffs and Trade (GATT), and other organizations designed to serve the interests of transnational corporations, banks, and investment firms.

One valuable feature of these organizations is their immunity from popular influence. Elite hostility to democracy is deep-rooted, understandably, but there has been a spectrum of opinion. At the "progressive" end, Walter Lippmann argued that "the public must be put in its place," so that the "responsible men" may rule without interference from "ignorant and meddlesome outsiders" whose "function" is to be only "interested spectators of action," periodically selecting members of the leadership class in elections, then returning to their private concerns. The statist reactionaries called "conservatives" typically take a harsher line, rejecting even the spectator role. Hence the appeal to the Reaganites of clandestine operations, censorship, and other measures to insure that a powerful and interventionist state will not be troubled by the rabble. The "new imperial age" marks a shift toward the reactionary end of the antidemocratic spectrum.

It is within this framework that the North American Free Trade Agreement (NAFTA) and GATT should be understood. Note first that such agreements have only a limited relation to free trade. One primary U.S. objective is increased protection for "intellectual property," including software, patents for seeds and drugs, and so on. The U.S. International Trade Commission estimates that American companies stand to gain $61 billion a year from the Third World if U.S. protectionist demands are satisfied by GATT (as they are in NAFTA), at a cost to the South that will dwarf the current huge flow of debt-service capital from South to North. Such measures are designed to insure that U.S.-based corporations control the technology of the future, including biotechnologies, which, it is hoped, will allow protected private enterprise to control health, agriculture, and the means of life generally, locking the poor majority into dependence and hopelessness. The same methods are being employed to undermine Canada's annoyingly efficient health services by imposing barriers to the use of generic drugs, thus sharply raising costs— and profits to state-subsidized U.S. corporations. NAFTA also includes intricate "rules of origin" requirements designed to keep foreign competitors out. Two hundred pages are devoted to rules to insure a high percentage of value added in North America (protectionist measures that should be increased, some U.S. opponents of NAFTA argue). Furthermore, the agreements go far beyond trade (itself not really trade but in large part intracompany transfers, as noted). A prime U.S. objective is liberalization of services, which would allow supranational banks to displace domestic competitors and thus eliminate any threat of national economic planning and independent development. The agreements impose a mixture of liberalization and protection, designed to keep wealth and power firmly in the hands of the masters of the "new imperial age."

NAFTA is an executive agreement, reached on 12 August 1992, just in time to become a major issue in the U.S. presidential campaign. It was mentioned, but barely. To give just one example of how debate was precluded, take the case of the Labor Advisory Committee (LAC), established by the Trade Act of 1974 to advise the executive branch on any trade

Manuel Sáenz. *Mexican children from Colonia Felipe Angeles play in one of the most contaminated areas of Cd. Juárez—on the border, near the premises of the U.S. company Asarco, which concentrates on the smelting of copper in El Paso.*

Above: Julián Cardona. *On 6 August 1997, Cd. Juárez police went a few feet into the U.S. on the Puente Interna-cional Zaragoza to break up a demonstration by farmers from Chihuahua. The anti-NAFTA demonstration was orga-nized by El Barzón, a national association that lends legal aid to its members, working to protect them from banks' unreasonable interest rates, which are especially harmful to Mexican farmers competing with subsidized U.S. farmers. Opposite:* Gabriel Cardona. *A production line in RCA Thomson, one of the first Cd. Juárez maquiladoras, estab-lished in the 1960s. The women work eight hours a day and often more. They earn the equivalent of about $4.50 a day. Many of them are single mothers who must leave their children alone while they work.*

agreement. The LAC, which is based in the unions, was informed that its report of NAFTA was due on September 9. The text of this intricate treaty was provided to it *one day before*. In its report, the LAC notes that, "the Administration refused to permit any outside advice on the development of this document and refused to make a draft available for comment." The situation in Canada and México was similar. The facts are not even reported. In such ways, we approach the long-sought ideal: formal democratic procedures that are devoid of meaning, as citizens not only do not intrude into the public arena but scarcely have an idea of the policies that will shape their lives.

One can readily understand the need to keep the public "in its place." Though the scanty press cov-erage is overwhelmingly favorable to NAFTA in its pre-sent form, the public opposes it by nearly two to one (of the 60 percent who have an opinion). Apart from some meager rhetoric and a few interventions by Ross Perot, that fact was irrelevant to the presiden-tial campaign, as were health reform and a host of other issues on which public opinion remains largely off the spectrum of options considered by the "responsible men."

The Labor Advisory Committee concluded that the executive treaty would be a bonanza for investors but would harm U.S. workers and probably Mexi-cans as well. One likely consequence is an accelera-tion of migration from rural to urban areas as Mexican corn producers are wiped out by U.S.

agribusiness, further depressing wages that have already dropped sharply in recent years and are likely to remain low, thanks to the harsh repression that is a crucial element of the highly touted Mexican "economic miracle." Labor's share of personal income in México declined from 36 percent in the mid-1970s to 23 percent by 1992, reports economist David Barkin, while fewer than 8,000 accounts (including 1,500 owned by foreigners) control more than 94 percent of stock shares in public hands.

Property rights are well protected by NAFTA, the LAC analysts and others note, while workers' rights are ignored. The treaty is also likely to have harmful environmental effects, encouraging a shift of production to regions where enforcement is lax. NAFTA "will have the effect of prohibiting democratically elected bodies at [all] levels of government from enacting measures deemed inconsistent with the provisions of the agreement," the LAC report continues, including those of the environment, workers' rights, and health and safety, all open to challenge as "unfair restraint of trade."

Such developments are already underway in the framework of the U.S.-Canada "free trade" agreement. Included are efforts to require Canada to abandon measures to protect the Pacific salmon, to bring pesticide and emissions regulations in line with laxer U.S. standards, to end subsidies for replanting after logging, and to bar a single-payer auto insurance plan in Ontario that would cost U.S. insurance companies hundreds of millions of dollars in profits. Meanwhile, Canada has charged the United States with violating "fair trade" by imposing EPA standards on asbestos use and requiring recycled fiber in newsprint. Under both NAFTA and GATT, there are endless options

Opposite top: Jaime Bailleres. *Mexican farmers demonstrate on the Puente Internacional Paso del Norte, asking the U.S. Congress not to approve NAFTA.*
Opposite bottom: Julián Cardona. *Julián Alvarado Fierro, the leader of the Sindicato de Choferes (the union of tractor-trailer-truck drivers, which is affiliated with the Partido Revolucionario Institucional, PRI—Institutional Revolutionary Party, long México's governing political party), was gunned down in front of the union's local headquarters.*

for undermining popular efforts to protect conditions of life.

In general, the LAC report concludes, "U.S. corporations, and the owners and managers of these corporations, stand to reap enormous profits. The United States as a whole, however, stands to lose and particular groups stand to lose an enormous amount." The report calls for renegotiation, offering a series of constructive proposals. That remains a possibility if the coalition of labor, environmental, and other popular groups that has been calling for such changes gains sufficient popular support [see Amy Lowrey and David Corn, "Mexican Trade Bill: Fast Track to Unemployment," *The Nation*, 3 June 1991].

An October 1992 report from the Congressional Office of Technology Assessment reached similar conclusions. A "bare" NAFTA of the form now on the table would ratify "the mismanagement of economic integration" and could "lock the United States into a low-wage, low-productivity future." Radically altered to incorporate "domestic and continental social policy measures and parallel understandings with México on environmental and labor issues," NAFTA could have beneficial consequences for the country. But the country is only of secondary concern to the masters, who are playing a different game. Its rules are revealed by what *The New York Times* called "Paradox of '92: Weak Economy, Strong Profits." As a geographical entity, "the country" may decline. But the interest of the "principal architects" of policy will be "mostly peculiarly attended to."

One consequence of the globalization of the economy is the rise of new governing institutions to serve the interests of private transnational economic power. Another is the spread of the Third World social model, with islands of enormous privilege in a sea of misery and despair. A walk through any American city gives human form to statistics on quality of life, distribution of wealth, poverty and employment, and other elements of the "Paradox of '92." Increasingly, production can be shifted to high-repression, low-wage areas and directed to privileged sectors in the global economy. Large parts of the population thus become superfluous for production and perhaps even as a market, unlike the days when Henry Ford realized that he could not sell cars unless his workers were paid well enough to buy cars themselves.

Particular cases fill out the picture. GM is planning to close almost two dozen plants in the United States and Canada, but it has become the largest private employer in México. It has also opened a $690 million assembly plant in eastern Germany, where employees are willing to "work longer hours than their pampered colleagues in western Germany," at 40 percent of the wage and with few benefits, as the *Financial Times* cheerily explains. Capital can readily move; people cannot, or are not permitted to by those who selectively applaud Adam Smith's doctrines, which crucially include "free circulation of labor." The return of much of Eastern Europe to its traditional service role offers new opportunities for corporations to reduce costs, thanks to "rising unemployment and pauperisation of large sections of the industrial working class" in the East as capitalist reforms proceed, according to the *Financial Times*.

The same factors provide the masters with new weapons against the rabble at home. Europe must "hammer away at high wages and corporate taxes, short working hours, labor immobility, and luxurious social programs," *Business Week* warns. It must learn the lesson of Britain, which finally "is doing something well," the *Economist* observes approvingly, with "trade unions shackled by law and subdued," "unemployment high," and the Maastricht social chapter rejected so that employers are protected "from over-regulations and under-flexibility of labour." American workers must absorb the same lessons.

The basic goals were lucidly described by the CEO of United Technologies, Harry Gray, quoted in a valuable study of NAFTA by William McGaughey of the Minnesota Fair Trade Coalition: "a worldwide business environment that's unfettered by government interference" (for example, "package and labeling requirements" and "inspection procedures" to protect consumers). This is the predominant human value, to which all else must be subordinated. Gray does not, of course, object to "government interference" of the kind that allows his corporation, an offshoot of the Pentagon system, to exist. Neoliberal rhetoric is to be selectively employed as a weapon against the poor; the wealthy and powerful will continue to rely upon state power.

These processes will continue independently of NAFTA. But, as explained by Eastman Kodak chairman Kay Whitmore, the treaty may "lock in the opening of México's economy so it can't go back to its protectionist ways." It should enable México "to solidify its remarkable economic reforms," comments Michael Aho, director of Economic Studies at the Council on Foreign Relations, referring to the "economic miracle" for the rich that has devastated the poor majority. It may fend off the danger noted by a Latin American Strategy Development Workshop at the Pentagon in September 1990, which found current relations with the Mexican dictatorship to be "extraordinarily positive," untroubled by stolen elections, death squads, endemic torture, scandalous treatment of workers and peasants, and so on, but which saw one cloud on the horizon: "a 'democracy opening' in México could test the special relationship by bringing into office a government more interested in challenging the U.S. on economic and nationalistic grounds." As always, the basic threat is a functioning democracy.

The trade agreements override the rights of workers, consumers, and the future generations who cannot "vote" in the market on environmental issues. They help keep the public "in its place." These are not necessary features of such agreements, but they are natural consequences of the great successes of the past years in reducing democracy to empty forms, so that the vile maxim of the masters can be pursued without undue interference.

(Originally written in 1993.)

Gabriel Cardona. *Backed-up traffic moving from Cd. Juárez to El Paso on the Puente Internacional Córdova-Américas (also known as the Puente Libre). Inspection by U.S. officials can sometimes make crossing the bridge into the U.S. take over an hour. To drive from El Paso to Cd. Juárez usually takes fifteen minutes or less.*

The notorious political apathy of Mexicans is intimately related to their all too obvious amorality, to their feeling of indifference and helplessness at the mere thought of combating any form of injustice. To depoliticize a nation is not simply to convince all its citizens of the futility of concerning themselves with public affairs, of the inexorable nature of the decision-making process, since no sort of collective pressure can be brought to bear on it. To depoliticize a nation is not simply to make the administration of the country a magical process resulting from deliberations behind the scene that take place every six years. It is also to deprive an entire country of the possibility of making moral choices, of the possibility of express-ing its indignation. It means destroying morality as a collective concern and reducing it to the status of an individual problem. It means death of a social morality and the encouragement of a petite bourgeoisie morality based on the need to create taboos, whereas any genuine morality is based on the ability to make free choices.

Carlos Monsiváis, in *Siempre!*, April 1968

JUÁREZ
THE LABORATORY OF OUR FUTURE

CHARLES BOWDEN

---

1. A SMALL NOTE: Riding the A Train on the Long Hot Night of Summer

The old man is getting on eighty and he crouches over the VCR trying to pounce on the right section of tape. His video collection features the underbelly part of Juárez, where drugs move, people die, bribes grace the palm. The room is very safe, walls

studded with family portraits, the smell of hot food wandering the air. On the screen, Amado Carrillo Fuentes, at that moment the boss of bosses in the Mexican drug world, officiates at his sister's wedding. She is very fat, Carrillo (or someone the authorities claim is Carrillo) is very tired, dark sagging patches under his eyes, the tie loose, the white shirt rumpled. Perhaps he suspected as the camcorder rolled in January of 1997 that he would be dead within six months. The next tape flares up with loud and friendly Mexican music as a crowd celebrates the birthday of Amado Carrillo Fuentes' ten-year-old son. The images are off handed. Suddenly, his three little daughters are dancing on the screen in a fine room with huge wooden armoires. Their bodies are tiny, their smiles delicious.

All this is accepted as a footnote to history. Anything bad in this world is seen as an aberration or as minor or not seen at all. This is proof positive of the hold the past has on our addiction, and our addiction is to rational thought based on rational models.

Globally, criminal drug cartels are now estimated to handle 8 percent of international trade. Globally, free trade is thriving as we tote up numbers of import and export, pat our sleek hips and congratulate ourselves on downsizing, study the overnight market reports and see fantastic gains in wealth for one and all.

I cannot prove that the numbers and the models and the projections are false. I can only describe the room and the evening and the rumble as the A train hurls toward the future. And it is a very safe and warm room as the summer night roasts the city and the air hangs like velvet from the sky. The pieces of the puzzle are now present. The warm embrace of family, the sure feel of the walls, the old man with his collection of clips of mayhem. Across the room in the reclining chair sits a friend and each day he goes to Juárez and installs equipment in yet one more new *maquiladora*. He is currently stuffing a plant with the equivalent of 7 million dollars' worth of tables and chairs and desks. Clearly, a boom is reverberating across this economically high-performing ground. He tells me that the old wreck in front of the house is for work so that it will not be stolen.

The couple is something else. They are in their early thirties, they are cops, and they are married with children. For almost a year now they have lived in their nice, warm home surrounded by ten-foot walls and concertina wire, the whole sanctuary panned by relentless video cameras. Of course, they are armed at all times—the man as he talks to me in the comfort of the family living room wears a .45 strapped to his hip. The woman has bright eyes and states her case firmly and clearly. There was a contract to take her husband's father to Juárez and skin him alive. The contract came from the world of Amado Carrillo Fuentes. The reason is unclear, they are puzzled by the absence of a readily understood motive, but it hardly matters now; they are in play and they know it. The authorities are of little or no use to them because they have stumbled into a world the governments know of but prefer to pretend does not exist. I watch the light dance in the woman's eyes as her words come out flat and even and matter-of-fact. She is resigned to her reality. As we sit and talk, Amado Carrillo Fuentes will be dead within a month, but this fact also hardly matters. Her father-in-law, in order to save his life, has been shipped overseas by the U.S. government. It is hoped this puts him beyond the reach of the world of Amado Carrillo Fuentes.

But what strikes me as I listen to the couple is the flow of my day. I have looked at hundreds of recent photographs from Juárez, many of which you will never see because they lack the right light or proper focus or are not perfectly framed. But mainly because there is a limit to how much we can stomach, and that goes for you and that goes for me. One photograph in particular keeps taking over my mind as I try to listen to the woman: in this image a young woman, eighteen, nineteen, twenty, I can't say for sure, lies on the ground stone-dead. Her face is clearly visible and it is caked with streams of fresh blood. A rock, and a good-sized rock, has been stuffed in her mouth, and now her lips look like an inner tube wrapped around the rock. You can hear her teeth breaking. So I try to listen to the woman over the sound of the teeth breaking.

I mention all this—the old man playing his video clips in the sanity of the family home, my friend talking about the big sale and installation of office furniture in yet one more foreign-owned factory in Juárez, the two married cops telling of their new life in a self-designed fort, the photograph of the dead girl silenced by stone—because I am just like you, I constantly take all these things and push them to the edge of my mind and tell myself they are freakish and marginal and not what life or the future or much of anything is about. Why just this very morning I was explaining to someone right here on the border the proper proportions for correctly mixing hummingbird food and daydreaming about planting epiphyllums in my garden.

But my mind's wanderings are brought up short by the woman who now lives in the fort, the woman who carries a badge and a gun but knows she is out there alone and society as she once imagined it has now vanished from her reality.

She looks at me and says, "None of this seems real until it happens to you."

That is when I hear the roar of the A train knifing through the warm velvet of the hot summer night and making a blood-red tear across the sky.

Pages 22–23: Manuel Sáenz. *In Cd. Juárez, excess waste is often burned in secret dumps, releasing toxic fumes into the air. The authorities have yet to deal with this environmental threat.*
Pages 26–27: Jaime Bailleres. *La Plaza de Armas, the main square in Cd. Juárez, and behind it La Catedral de Ciudad Juárez and La Misión de Guadalupe.*

CUANDO LAS MASAS DESPIERTAN LA REVOLUCION

2. THERE IS A MAN ON A ROCK

First come the whispers. The river brushes the shore, faintly stirring the reeds as I look south into México at the outskirts of Juárez, and from this caress a soft sound rises up from the slick waters. A body floats up big with gas, a sixteen-year-old boy who has been a day or two or three on the bottom and now breaks the surface.

Everybody hates floaters, the way the flesh can tear away when you take them out of the water. They fetched him out very near here. The July air is heavy with dreams of rain and the river runs big as dams let loose a heavy flow for fields far downstream. What is needed at this moment is imagination. First, imagine the drowning, the thrashing in the dark waters and then the arms and the head slipping beneath the surface. Next, imagine that the green fields across the river are a different nation called México. Finally, imagine that this brooding snake of water, the Rio Grande to those on the north bank, the Rio Bravo to the people on the south shore, imagine it is a line on the world's maps dividing one nation from another.

Right at this moment the river is whispering as it flows through the cattails, the purring of the waters spiked by the coarse sound of blackbirds clinging to the green stalks of the marsh plants. There is a dirt track on a dike right behind me where the Border Patrol squats in trucks every few hundred yards waiting for them to try and come north. Here and there are huge portable floodlights borrowed from the military to aid in the night work. The Mexican newspapers say El Paso firemen towed the body to shore and that the local county coroner examined it and declared the boy dead.

Manuel Sáenz. *The body of a murdered coyote found by U.S. authorities.*

I drive to the main fire station, an antiseptic building that reeks of order, and the personnel hit their keyboards, run their machines, and give me pages of printout itemizing every call in that sector of the river on the day the body rose up from the dark bottom of mud. I stand in the big lobby of the main station and the polished floor, the patient and helpful staff, the whooshing of the air conditioners all conspire to make me believe in order and rules. The dead boy is not on the list. The Mexican report that he was fished out by U.S. authorities is at best a fantasy. I visit the coroner, a nervous and fleshy man who seems alarmed by the idea of any questions about anything. And no, he says, he did some floaters in July, but not this one, not a sixteen-year-old boy.

Why do you want to know? he asks.

I do not tell him the truth. I say I am just curious.

I'll tell you. I keep hearing in my head this line from Carl Sandburg, "I tell you the past is a bucket of ashes." I love this line and do not believe it. I'm here because the past is alive. I want to know about the river, about the imaginary line, about the green fields next to the big dusty Mexican city of Juárez. I want to know about *over there*. I want to know the smell of the streets at 2 A.M., the taste of the whore under the streetlight, the greasy feel of the juice rolling down my chin from the taco bought at a stand near dawn. I want to beat on a drum the cadence of the city, the habitual rhythm that bops the people through their day and into the night. The factory is letting

Above: Gabriel Cardona. *A Tarahumara girl and her little brother in Colonia Tarahumara, Cd. Juárez. Colonia Tarahumara, which is in an elevated part of the city, gets cold in winter, sometimes even experiencing snowstorms, but many of the homes there have no doors. To stay warm, people often start wood fires, although their homes, too, are made of wood or even cardboard—easily flammable materials.*

Right: Gabriel Cardona. *Colonia Universidad, one of the poorest colonias in Cd. Juárez. Most houses are one room, and must often accommodate more than one family.*

loose a shift, and hundreds pour out the doors and trudge down neighboring dirt lanes toward cardboard shacks, and I want to go home with them and turn on the radio, eat some beans, and feel the fatigue in every cell. I want to feel the power of a .45 automatic tucked inside the belt of a paunchy Mexican federal cop as he sits in the hotel bar staring me down with contempt and malice. There is more but you get the idea: across the river and into the flesh. The body is going to tell me these things. It is my bloated, rotting, cold Rosetta stone fragrant with the stench of corruption.

After days of searching I find the mother of the dead boy. She has been moving steadily through the rougher barrios of Juárez. Her husband tried to strangle her, one of her children is in an American prison

Pages 32–33: Gabriel Cardona. *A fire consumed ten houses in Colonia México 68. Fires are common in the colonias' cardboard-and-wood houses, which are often illuminated by candles and heated by wood fires set directly on the floor. The residents sometimes try to connect their homes to the city's electrical system, but in doing so they risk short circuits that can also cause fires. Here, a father tries to save his house with a little garden hose. He's lucky. Many of the colonias have no regular water supply, making the inevitable fires virtually impossible to extinguish.*

Right: Manuel Sáenz. *Some of the poorest families in Juárez live in the city's many dumps, competing with animals for scraps of food, or anything else useful.*

for murder, two others under the age of ten cling to her dress, and yes, she says, her sixteen-year-old is dead. She is in her early or mid-thirties, the eyes hard and yet flickering with fright. White people mean danger to her. She says the day her son vanished under the waters, three boys came to her who had been trying to sneak into the U.S. with her son. They said he slipped or something, the current took him, and then he vanished and drowned. I nod. Then she says her sister either saw the body or talked to the people who put it in its casket, and her sister told her that the boy's head had been bashed in and there were other signs of violence. I nod. Now she is a fugitive from her hard-drinking and murderous husband, from the shack that she can no longer sleep in, and from hunger. She sells used clothing in the street and makes, she guesses, the equivalent of $15 a week. This night she has taken refuge in a barrio named Colonia Tierra y Libertad—Land and Liberty, the battle cry of Emiliano Zapata. I give her money and

Above: Julián Cardona. *An elderly member of the Sociedad Cooperativa de Seleccionadores de Materiales (Cooperative society for selectors of materials) collects cardboard boxes and other materials that he will later sell.*
Opposite: Javier Aguilar. *Constructed in 1997 by the U.S. Border Patrol as part of Operation Hold the Line, this metal fence divides Sunland Park, New Mexico, from the Colonia Puerto de Anapra, Cd. Juárez.*
Pages 38–39: Gabriel Cardona. *Before operations Border Blockade and Hold the Line, Mexicans working in El Paso would cross the Rio Grande regularly and openly in rubber tubes with the help of* lancheros, *who would charge the equivalent of $2 for the trip. A lanchero is hired only for the crossing of the river; a coyote can be hired to take a client across the border and to a specific destination, charging anywhere from twenty dollars to several hundred; a* pollero *brings groups of people across.*

she leaves near midnight to buy milk and cereal for the children.

But I keep on with this matter and one night I am sitting with a Mexican reporter who says yes, I saw photographs taken of the body in the Juárez morgue.

The hands and feet were tied, the body black and blue from a beating—particularly around the crotch—and a stout piece of cable constricted the neck. I finger the Mexican autopsy report, a one-page touchstone of order, and this report says the cause of death was drowning. No matter, these variations on a theme occur and I have grown to accept them. After that, I talk to a photographer who saw the body come out of the river and took photographs. He describes the condition of the sixteen-year-old boy in much the same way as the reporter. He says he has negatives should I wish to see them.

Yes, yes, I allow, I'd kind of like to look at them. We agree on a price and the night rolls on. That was some time ago. I still do not have the photographs, neither the ones taken in the morgue nor the ones taken as the bloated body was fished out of the river. It is unfinished business, a condition that is endemic on this line between nations. But that is how I stumbled into the photographers of Juárez and into the bowels of Juárez and into the world that peers out from this book. I began to imagine. And after I began to imagine, I argued with the things I saw in my mind. And after I tired of arguing, I finally began to see. The boy floating in the river where the waters whisper through the cattails is one little story, a tale still

Opposite top: Ernesto Rodríguez. *With few established, affordable educational facilities in Cd. Juárez, school is often taught in makeshift outdoor environments where students must endure extreme weather conditions. On this June 1997 day in Colonia Toribio Ortega, temperatures rose to 104 degrees during schooltime.*
Opposite bottom: Julián Cardona. *A canal of* aguas negras *(contaminated water, such as untreated sewage, or waste water from the maquiladoras) separates one of the ca. 325 maquiladoras in Cd. Juárez—this one in the Rio Bravo industrial park (in the background)—from the new home of seven-year-old Guadalupe Valenzuela Rosales, who lives with her parents, two sisters, and brother in a cardboard-and-wood house. Her family and many of their neighbors came to Cd. Juárez from the southern states of Coahuila and Durango in search of employment and better living conditions. In 1997, a fire razed ten of these houses and also the wooden bridges that cross the canal to the Rio Bravo industrial park, where Guadalupe's family and their neighbors work.*

unfinished that will find its conclusion in a different time and place. This book is about other stories that occur over there, across the river. The comfortable way to deal with these other stories is to say they are about them. The way to understand these other stories is to say they are about us. I was born into the second way.

You are running down a dark street, you left the car door flung open when you lurched out and smelled the cool pavement of night smearing your face, and you are very alive as you race toward someone very dead. You are a cop, you are a reporter, you are a photographer, you are a man, you are a woman. You are tasting something we seldom talk about: horror slapping our systems awake and making us feel more alive than the gardens we cultivate with love during the better hours. Juárez is a depressing place and Juárez makes us feel more alive. Later over drinks, we can speak of a mission, and we can believe those words because those words are true. But still we know something else also drives us—the rush of life exploding from its hidden and underground rivers and suddenly roaring around us as we make notes and we take photographs and we listen, and, oh my God, do we feel alive amid the screams. In the academies they have sessions bemoaning this reality. In the streets, they are simply lived. I believe that Juárez is one of the most exciting places in the world. I am struck by the electricity that snaps through the air in a city saturated with grief. And so we will come to know photographers trying to change the world with cameras while working all the while amid pain and cruelty and poverty and sadness. And laughing and surging with energy as they work. We should accept this tension between the desire for peace and quiet, and the excitement of mayhem. We all experience this sensation as we slow down and stare at the bad car wreck on the highway. And so we will come to know ourselves, a people of gardens with one foot on the third rail.

There is a family in Juárez I know casually. They figure slightly in the pages that follow and are named Carranza. I first met them in April of 1996 and since then have periodically dropped by their shack in a

Juárez squatter's community called Anapra. When I first saw them, the teenage girls, all working in American factories, were bright-eyed and glowing. As the months slid past, there were changes. I remember dropping by with a cake for the sixteenth birthday of one of the girls. Her face was wan, the eyes tired, the movements languid. It was her day off. She smiled feebly at the cake, and as the family gathered around under a gray winter sky, they all had the air of the beaten. I could sense they were losing, being worn down. Of course, this was just an impression. But everything begins as impressions and some things end as they begin.

I think often about the Carranza family. I can taste the wind, feel the cool gray air of winter, see the girl staring down at the cake and feel in my bones the fatigue slowly growing in her young body. I am looking at a photo of her as I type these words. I remem-

ber that for a while she and her sisters thought I kept coming around with a friend because we were looking for sex. She explained this fact to us one day. She said no one had ever helped them, so they had assumed we must be after their bodies. We said nothing. Sometimes there is nothing to say.

I live in a time of vast, raucous entertainments and great silence. The things I see on the streets seem unreal, the images on the screen in my motel room feel solid, sure, and true. It reminds me of being drugged in the '60s. Only now I am straight and the sense of disorientation is yet stronger. Juárez does not compute with what I read and hear. But few daily, humdrum things seem connected to the vast underpinnings of my time. It is as if knowledge and everyday life have been severed. Science is heavily funded and yet does not seem consciously to impinge on the way people live, think, or die.

In my lifetime, the secure belief that a rational world was in the control of the planet and its population, and that this rational world could handily manipulate numbers and forces, has been undermined by three scientific insights. One was the construct of the DNA's double helix in the '50s. This new idea had many consequences, and the stock market is studded with avaricious companies hoping to capitalize on it by tinkering with the structure of life to create more profitable life forms. But the deeper consequence of the double helix was and is to burn into human consciousness the fact that the past is not merely a rumor or quiet talk but a template of vast complexity commingled in every living thing. The dead hand can never again be seen as dead, but as a living information system busily mutating beneath our consciousness, our level of knowledge, and our control. We can never simply escape history since, down to the very cells in our body, we *are* history. The second great scientific insight was the eruption of the idea that the world moved: tectonic plates. We ride on skateboards that careen around a planet still actively designing its surface shape and appearance. The planet writhes and is not a finished thing. The rock can betray us by scampering away, and nothing under our feet can ever be taken for granted. The seas rise, drown us, and then in turn recede. No more faiths will be so naively erected with the phrase "Upon this rock." Finally, there is the matter of chaos theory, which tells us that the world has form and pattern but that knowing the forms and patterns does not enable us confidently to predict the next form or pattern. Chaos theory takes us back to the Greek philosopher dipping his foot into the river of constant change. All three of these insights at first caused consternation and were in some instances almost suppressed and circulated through a kind of scholarly samizdat. All three have essentially triumphed in the academy and been largely ignored in the worlds of politics, economics, and social planning. It seems to me that this feat has a heavy price. It blinds us not only to the disintegration of empires but to the erosion of the traditional state. The talk of a new world order is akin to a fool trying to whistle past a cemetery.

Opposite and right: Gabriel Cardona. *Two of the many people who must survive on the streets in Cd. Juárez.*
Page 44 top: Lucio Soria Espino. *This woman has lived in an abandoned bus in Cd. Juárez for the past five years.*
Page 44 bottom: Ernesto Rodríguez. *As the distributors of water in Cd. Juárez only come through the poorer colonias two or three times a month, people must buy water to store, sometimes in metal drums that may be contaminated from previous use as maquiladoras' storage containers for chemicals.*
Page 45 top: Gabriel Cardona. *A blaze caused by the unprotected fires used for cooking destroyed the home of this Tarahumara woman and her family in Colonia El Mirador long before the firemen arrived. Not only is water in limited supply in many of the colonias, the fire department stations are sometimes too far away to arrive promptly.*
Page 45 bottom: Jaime Bailleres. *A fire destroyed seventy-five cardboard-and-wood homes in Colonia Universidad, inhabited mostly by members of the Comité de Defensa Popular (CDP—Committee for popular defense). "Nobody knows" the cause of the fire, but inhabitants search through the ashes for remains and reusable materials so they may rebuild their homes.*
Pages 46–47: Julián Cardona. *Hosiery discarded by El Paso shopkeepers is bought, mended, dyed, and dried in the sun by a Cd. Juárez woman living in Colonia Puerto de Anapra, who then resells the stockings for the equivalent of about $1.*

We have endured a century of efforts to ride herd on the beast within us through various economic philosophies that used the state as a bludgeon. Over vast swatches of the earth, our voices were throttled because the structure of government became something more than jolly town halls or tribal councils and for the first time not only sought to control our behavior but, thanks to technology, increasingly had the means to attempt the engineering of thought. Where slaves had always given up their bodies, the new rulers wished also to shackle our minds. All the variations of state corporatism—communism, capitalism, fascism, socialism—shifted from being forms of social expression to being fists for social control. Some of us were force-fed the thoughts of the Chair-

man, some of us were trained to piss into cups at the workplace. This dreary legacy is known to all of us. What must be considered is why these efforts failed and what is driving the world that shreds these efforts.

These systems fell or are falling—right now the problems of the modern state are best seen not as a contest between the quick and the dead but as a scene where some states die more swiftly than others—because the resources that fed them are declining. There may no longer be enough cheap available energy for the state as we have known it. What we now see in Juárez is a sign of this. Here, transnational corporations, the new and inventive substitutes for governments and empires, make a stand against the growing and violent future in order to maintain profits by beating down labor. Juárez is a new and invigorating charnel house erected by a dying order. And its ferocity can be seen on the faces of the family Carranza, or in the thousands of dull-eyed workers spilling out of Third World factories after a long, ill-paid shift.

It can be felt upon the skin. It can be a scent rising from the ground. It can be the crack of a gun in the dark night. Always, it is the constant sound that any jumble of a city throws off from its loves and labors. More than sixteen million machines cross the river at Juárez each year and they all talk with or without mufflers at every hour of the day and night. The trains cross the river also and the people come and go, whether with the law at their backs or in their faces. Life collects in this place, just as it grows noisy and electric in a swamp.

Anyone who has looked into an ecosystem has found points where life is amplified, where all the flora and fauna grow thick and vocal because of factors of light, water, temperature, and soil, and where the sheer weight of protoplasm leaps and celebrates. Juárez is such a place, where two nominal worlds, México and the United States, reach startlingly large and strange forms. If this city were some New England settlement with its skies punctured by Congregational churches, town halls, and swatches of village greens, it would still command our attention simply because of its sheer vitality. What I am saying is: if Juárez were functional and clean and a model for all the nations, we would still be fascinated by it. But Juárez is not functional, it is not orderly, and it is not pretty. It has the throb and drive of nineteenth-century Chicago, the most significant human community on the planet following the American Civil War, yet commands the attention of some nameless suburb of real life. We do not wish to look at Juárez, we do not vacation there, we do not speak of the place. When it briefly comes to our attention, we dismiss it as a grotesque exception to what matters, what is, and what will be. We believe or profess to believe that the present and the future are more palpable in cyberspace than on the ground by the river that divides the United States from México. This is an opinion I do not share.

I have been a hunch player all of my life. In the '60s, I sensed that the center of human energy had shifted to shacks in the Mississippi Delta, where poor black people were achieving what American presidents and congresses could not dream would ever be possible. These things happen contrary to the official records. Just as at times in the '60s anyone could sense that more power and energy were pouring out of electric guitars than out of cannons, a fact that almost toppled governments on several continents in the year 1968. In the '70s, I put my chips on the edges and left the great cities and universities of my nation for the impossible backlands. In ecology there is the concept of the ecotone, that borderland between two biological assemblages—think of the forest edging the meadow. Where an ecotone occurs there is more life and life is louder and more grasping because two or more groups of plants and animals overlap, boosting life's pitch and intensity. Every naturalist knows this and every successful hunter stalks these zones. That is what is happening now on the border of México and the United States, where a huge ecotone of flesh and capital and guns is rubbing up against itself as two cultures and two economies and two languages

Margarita Reyes. *Tarahumara children prepare their meal outdoors near a working-class district on the outskirts of Cd. Juárez.*

meet and mingle and erupt into something we cannot yet name.

At the beginning of this century, the border of México and the United States was almost a nothing to both nations. Now it is a scream that disturbs the sleep of the rulers in their various palaces. Think of Juárez as a land-locked Hong Kong in the dry desert winds. I have a hunch about Juárez, and my hunch is that this ignored place offers the real "Windows" on the coming times. The future has a way of coming from the edges, of being created not in the central plaza but on the blurry fringes of our peripheral vision. Mongols on horses come out of the blank of the grasslands, boys and girls in garages invent a toy called the personal computer and bring huge corpo-

rations to their knees, a virus mutates in Africa and wreaks havoc on the love life of the planet. A workday begins in Ciudad Juárez, Chihuahua, México, just across the river from El Paso, Texas, U.S.A.

Juárez haunts me and yet I spend much of my time deliberately trying to erase it from my mind. It is the book I repeatedly close.

And then reopen. More than a century ago, Fyodor Dostoyevsky, that most Mexican of writers, said clearly what little I have learned:

I have my own particular opinions about the real. What most call fantastic and impossible is often for me real in its actual and deepest meaning—the true reality. A record of everyday events is for me far from realism, rather it is the opposite. In every single newspaper, you can find stories about absolutely real yet absolutely strange facts that our writers would

Above: Ernesto Rodríguez. *Children play in a tub of dirty water outside a house that served as a voting office during elections in July 1997.*

Opposite: Ernesto Rodríguez. *A little girl, one of hundreds of street children who work from a very young age in order to survive, takes a short siesta in the trash after selling items on the Puente Internacional Paso del Norte for most of the day. Exposure to both the intense sun and the toxic fumes emitted by the thousands of vehicles that cross the bridges between El Paso and Cd. Juárez is enormously harmful to the children.*

Pages 52–53: Miguel Perea. *A Mexican trying to cross the Rio Grande and enter the U.S. without proper documents holds his clothes to keep them from getting wet.*

reject and call fantastic—these things hold no interest for them. And yet these stories are the deep and living reality, because they are facts. They happen every day, every moment; they are in no way exceptional.

I'll tell you one more story that takes place over there, not in Juárez but far away in the Sea of Cortés, that thin trough of water separating the Mexican mainland from Baja California. About halfway up, the midriff islands rise above the waters and stretch like a necklace across the ten-thousand-foot-deep tongue of ocean. Temporary fishing camps dot these islands from which men in open boats put out each day to cast their nets and pray for fish. A man comes to one of these camps and in the story no one really knows from what part of México he ventured forth. He is very poor, he is terrified of sharks, he cannot swim. He has no boat, he owns no net. So each morning when the fishermen put out, they take him to a rock that barely pokes above the sea and leave him there with a line to try and catch some fish. At high tide the rock disappears underwater. The man stands there—sometimes in the story he stands on one leg like a stork and casts his line and waits all day for the fishermen to return and retrieve him before the ocean takes the rock down once again. The outboard motors on the fishing boats constantly break down and it is a commonplace to see them bobbing on the swells as a fisherman curses and tinkers and tries to get the engine fired up again. Also, in summer, sudden storms come up and often capsize and drown the men who work in the small open boats. It is a hard life for those who can find no life at all on the land. When I think of this story of the man on the rock, all these things—the sharks, the storms, the busted-down boats, the inability to swim, the tides—come to the fore in my mind. And I share his peril for a few seconds.

Of course, the story comes to me third- or fourth-hand and maybe it is true and maybe it is not. But it won't go away because it says what I sense when I cross the river. I am sitting in a nice bar holding a glass of good wine and the talk around me is all in Spanish and the food is very fine and just outside the building the streets roar with traffic and buses blow black exhaust and trucks fire without mufflers, and I see the man on the rock. He is standing there with a line and the tides are rising. I see him everywhere in Juárez. I also see the sharks ceaselessly circling. Sometimes, now, I see the man in the mirror when I shave.

First come the whispers. Across the river. A man standing on a rock.

It is the instability of Mexico which is maddening:
a land so rich, so beautiful; a race, the Indians, so
tender, lovable; but all smeared over with a slime
of political intrigue and treachery in which my own
country has played its shameful part.

Edward Weston, *The Daybooks*, 12 June 1924

3. THERE IS A WHITE LIGHT

The white eye of the blank screen waits in the dark room. A few moments ago Jaime Bailleres was nuzzling his thirteen-month-old child and walking around in the calm of his apartment. His wife Graciela puttered in the kitchen and soft words and laugh-ter floated through the serenity of their home. A copy of a work on semiotics lay on the coffee table and the rooms say culture and civility and the joy of ideas. Outside, Cd. Juárez, Chihuahua, waited with sharp teeth. Now the lights are off as Jaime Bailleres dances through a carousel of slides.

I am here because of a seventeen-year-old girl. The whole thing started very simply. I was drinking black coffee and reading the Juárez paper and there tucked away in the back pages, where the small crimes of the city bleed for a few inches, I saw her face. She was smiling at me and wore a strapless gown riding on breasts powered by an uplift bra, and a pair of fancy gloves reached above her elbows almost to her armpits. The story said she'd disappeared, all 1.6 meters of her.

I turned to a friend I was having breakfast with and said what's this about?

He replied matter-of-factly, Oh, they disappear all the time. Guys kidnap them, rape them, and kill them.

Pages 54–55: Jaime Murrieta. *One of the more than 175,000 maquiladora workers in Cd. Juárez. Often these women leave their colonias for work in the early morning hours, sometimes having to walk many miles, and always risking an encounter with members of one of the gangs, or with one of the narcotraficantes who populate the streets after dark.*
Opposite: Manuel Sáenz. *A murdered maquiladora girl, one of many in Cd. Juárez who were kidnapped and murdered in 1996.*
Right: Jaime Bailleres. *The Queen of the Juegos Olímpicos Intermaquiladoras (Intermaquiladora Olympic games) walks in the parade that accompanies the games.*

Them?

Oh, he continued, you know, the young girls who work in the maquiladoras, the foreign-owned factories, the girls that have to leave for work when it is still dark. As a local fruit vendor told an American daily, "Even the devil is scared of living here." That's

when my interest in border photography quickened. I'd been idly pursuing that one photograph of a drowned sixteen-year-old—the teenager said to have been murdered before he took his last swim. When I started asking around I met the herd of photographers who work for the two Juárez dailies and a fistful of bloody tabloids and other rags. I was stunned by their work because I am an American and the photographs showed a world foreign and sharp-edged. I came here with basic baggage—a belief in civility, hard work, decent pay, suspicion of any government and all authority, and the certain faith that you fight power every day of your life and pay no attention to the scorecard but, rather, simply relish the battle. I am a creature of hope, a glass of wine in the evening, and music always in the air. Juárez is a city of violence, little hope, hundreds and hundreds of foreign

factories, sub-living wages, vivid colors, and gory moments. I was instantly seduced and struggled not at all. I decided to write about the photographers in order to get people to look and think about Juárez, in order to get past vague terms such as free trade, NAFTA, GATT, and the global village. It was and is as simple as that.

After that initial decision, smells and sounds and tastes and blurry facts took over and I spent over a year writing and pitching one simple story about one little group of street photographers in one border crossing in a world where borders are increasingly flashpoints between races, cultures, economies, and nations. I came with little theory but outfitted with a few rough beliefs I had learned before I was old enough to make my own living. I believe that if you work all day you should be able to buy enough grub

Above: Julián Cardona. *In 1995, 500 farmers and Indians from twenty Chihuahua agricultural municipalities demonstrated on the Puente Internacional Paso del Norte after holding a three-hour vigil in front of the U.S. Consulate in Cd. Juárez to ask for "economic asylum" for 15,000 of the state's farmers. These farmers believed that the Mexican federal government brought them to the brink of ruin, and they gave Consul Bryan Wilson a document arguing that "the Neoliberal economic policy, with its program of cutting subsidies, or price increases for machinery, seeds, fertilizers and other materials; of abolishing guaranteed prices; of raising interest rates; and of indiscriminately importing farm products from abroad has plunged the Mexican countryside into the worst crisis of its history."*

Opposite: Julián Cardona. *Victoria Acosta Alvarado is presented with flowers by schoolmates of her ten-year-old daughter, Cinthia Rocio Acosta, who was raped and murdered in the winter of 1997. The Policía Judicial del Estado (State judiciary police) responded to the crime by accusing Acosta Alvarado of negligence, a common accusation they make to justify their own alleged negligence.*

to feed you, have claim on enough space to shelter you, and live with enough security not to fear random violence or death. I believe a living wage means you can continue to live. That's about it. I am telling you all this because I do not have a general theory about how the world works—I lack the deep idiotic belief in the sanctity of communism, socialism, capitalism, and state corporatism. I simply demand that any belief system or power system meet my standards of sustenance, shelter, and moments of joy. If it does not, then the hell with it. I have never believed for one instant in John F. Kennedy's famous line about asking not what your country can do for you but what you can do for your country. If your country does not serve you, then why should it exist? Government has no purpose except to benefit its citizens. None.

Left: Lucio Soria Espino. *A classic narco execution, in which the victim is handcuffed and tortured.*
Below: Jaime Bailleres. *Pablo Rodríguez begs the paramedics to help his younger brother Ricardo, who has overdosed on heroin, but it is too late.*

So I wind up in a pleasant room with a glass of wine, surrounded by photographers, and I bathe in the flow of images. The photographers, like Jaime showing me his slides, are the next logical step in my effort to understand a place where beaming seventeen-year-old girls suddenly vanish. Juárez/El Paso constitutes one of the largest border communities on this earth, but hardly anyone seems to admit the Mexican side exists. Within this forgotten urban maze work some of the friskiest photographers still roaming the streets with 35mm cameras. I think that they are capturing something: the look of the future, and the future to me looks like the face of a murdered girl. This future is based on the rich getting richer, the poor getting poorer, and industrial growth producing poverty faster than it distributes wealth.

Until recently in México the workers got one-eighth the wages of their U.S. counterparts. Such generosity no longer prevails and wages now flutter somewhere between one-tenth and one-fifteenth of those in the U.S. In the auto industry, it looks like this: U.S. autoworkers at union plants average $16.75 per hour, Mexicans take home the equivalent of $4.50 per day. I realize this statement sketches something that sounds and looks like a cartoon. We prefer matters to be complex and qualified enough so that we can ignore them or dismiss them or, better yet, commission more studies and yet another meeting. I've been to this crossroads before, and, unlike the great blues man Robert Johnson, the devil has not made me an offer—the straight world has. Perhaps that is the modern version of Faust: the devil appears in a three-piece suit, or wearing a trim beard tacked onto a Ph.D., or smiling earnestly and saying Yes, yes, but what can we do about it?

At one point in my Juárez wanderings I go to a U.S. university television station to outline a documentary on free trade, factories, teenage laborers, bad deaths, good music, flashing smiles, and the soft curves of dunes dotted with bodies. I can see the producer and the on-camera talent glancing at each other as the air conditioner purrs and the fluorescent lights

hum overhead, and I know I am now the crazy person in this group. Or I am on the telephone to a New York magazine editor and I am outlining a possible story, one very much like the tale you now hold in your hands, and I can hear the hesitation give way to discomfort and finally land in embarrassment as the editor jockeys to escape the strangeness and vileness of what I want to say and how I want to say it. The story is too simple, their silences indicate, to be true, too cruel to be stomached, too near to have been missed. And too close for comfort.

We have these models in our heads about growth, development, infrastructure. Juárez doesn't look like any of these images, so our ability to see this city comes and goes—mainly goes. A nation that does not have jury trials, that has been dominated by one party (Partido Revolucionario Institucional, PRI—Institutional Revolutionary Party) for most of this century, that is carpeted with corruption and poverty and pockmarked with chancres called billionaires is touted as an emerging democracy marching toward First World standing. The snippets of fact that once in a great while percolate up through the Mexican press are ignored by the U.S. government and its citizens. México may be the last great drug experience for the American people, one in which reality gives way to pretty colors. So I come to the photos and the street shooters as a way to literally give people a picture of an economic world they cannot seem to acknowledge or comprehend. Juárez is not a backwater but the new City on the Hill, beckoning us all to a grisly state of things.

I've got my feet propped up on a coffee table, a glass of wine in my hand, and as far as the half-dozen photographers present for the slide show are concerned, this is my first day of school, and they're not sure if I've got what it takes to be a good student. After all, not many come here if they have a choice, and absolutely no one comes to view their work. The photographers of Juárez once put on an exhibition. No one in El Paso, separated from México by thirty feet of river, was interested in hanging their work, so they got a small room in Juárez and hung big prints they could not really afford to make. They called their show "*Nada qué ver,*" Nothing to see.

"We're getting closer to the events," Jaime explains. "We don't think we are artists because we have no people here who can tell us if this is art."

In the beginning was Héctor Oaxaca. He is seventy now and the godfather of the street shooters of Juárez. His favorite photo is this: a governor surrounded by his bodyguards has just learned that in México City the president has removed him from office. The governor, Héctor explained to me with

Opposite: Julián Cardona. *Police photograph evidence in the murder of a man who had been stabbed about thirty times. He was found on the territorial boundaries of the La Fama and Los Calaveras gangs, in Colonia 16 de Septiembre. In Cd. Juárez, an estimated 40 percent of the homicides in recent years can be attributed to gang violence.*
Below: Jaime Bailleres. *Sixteen-year-old gang member Rodolfo Velázquez Acosta, or El Topo (The Mole), is arrested in Colonia del Carmen, where he has shot seventeen-year-old Jesús Benítez almost to death.*

great pleasure, is weeping. After Oaxaca came Miguel Perea. He is a quiet man with the physical grace of a cat. For years he was a matador, but he left the safety of the bull ring for the electric dangers of the streets of Juárez. He is the conscience of the street shooters and has left his mark on their lens. He taught them that photographs could be social documents and that strong photographs could change the way people think and feel.

Beginning in the early '80s, some shooters began to show up with university degrees and tattered copies of the work of New York's famous street shooter, Weegee (Arthur Fellig). A tradition of gritty, unsentimental, and loving street-shooting that has all but perished in the United States was reborn in Juárez, in part because the newspapers offered a market. The street shooters are mainly young and almost always broke. Pay at the various newspapers runs from the equivalent of $50 to $100 a week and they must provide their own cameras and transportation

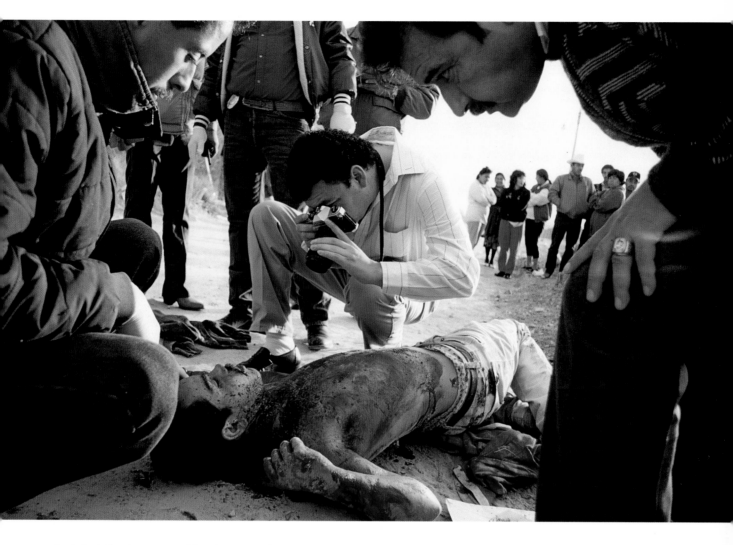

on the job. Film is rationed by their employers to cut expenses.

"We are like firemen," Jaime Bailleres explains, "only here we fight fires with our bare hands."

Sometimes newspeople get burned here. Ten years ago, the *federales* shot and killed local reporter Linda Bejarano, who was pregnant at the time, along with her mother and a friend. They said they mistook her for a drug dealer. In the early '90s, Dr. Victor Manuel Oropeza was a regular columnist for a Juárez newspaper. He wrote a series about connections between the federal police and the *narcotraficantes*. On 3 July 1991, his tortured body was found. The federal police quickly nailed some scoundrels. But their confessions were so blatantly produced by torture that México's attorney general's human rights officer, Teresa Jardí Alonso, resigned in protest.

The slide presentation clicks away. An empty bull-ring flares up on the screen and a sign below a green platform shouts in huge letters, "DIOS ESTÁ AQUÍ" (God is here). Jaime's friend Alfredo Carrillo stares intently at the images. He is twenty-one years old and until four months ago worked in radio. Alfredo is a well-set-up kid with quick eyes and a ravenous hunger for photos. Jaime is giving Alfredo tips on how to handle various light conditions and how to frame different scenes. A dead junkie lies on the sidewalk and his brother crouches over the body and weeps. A child of seven is pinned under a massive beam. He and his father were tearing apart a building for its old bricks when the ceiling collapsed. Jaime says that the child is whimpering and saying he is afraid of death. He lasted a few minutes more.

A hand reaches out from under a blanket—a cop cut down by AK-47s in front of a mansion owned by Amado Carrillo Fuentes as the police were checking out a van parked on the street. Carrillo was a local businessman. U.S. authorities calculate he moved more than one hundred tons of coke a year across the bridge and into El Paso. Carrillo was estimated to be earning the equivalent of $200 million a week, and to the joy of economists, this business is hard currency and cash-and-carry. To my untrained eye the dimensions of the dope business are simple: without it the Mexican economy would totally collapse. A gold ring gleams on the cop's dead hand; for Bailleres it is a study in the ways of power. Alfredo says, "All these young kids dream of being Amado Carrillo." He is not smiling when he says this.

The competition in this dreamland is rough. Yesterday, Juan Manuel Bueno Dueñas, twenty-three, got in a dispute with a drug dealer. He belonged to Los Harpys. Today at 4:30 P.M. he was buried in the municipal cemetery by his fellow gang members. The *campo santo* was crowded with people, the afterflow of the just-concluded Day of the Dead. Carloads of guys from Barrio Chico, rivals of Los Harpys, opened fire on the procession. No one is certain how many people were wounded. The death convulsions of the Mexican economy have left the young to their own devices. Since December 1994, the currency has lost over half its value, prices have more than doubled, and jobs have disappeared wholesale. Real numbers hardly exist—in México, for example, you are counted as employed if you work one hour a week. The government regularly announces that recovery is underway and regularly nothing happens in the lives of working people. The gangs of Juárez, *las pandillas*, kill up to 150 people a year. Accepting such realities is possible. Thinking about them is not. Survival in Juárez is based on alcohol, friendships, and laughter. But this happens in private. The streets are full of people wearing masks. Jaime was photographing a dog show at the time of the shooting in the cemetery. Now he and Alfredo sit in the safety of his home and laugh at the thought of these locos running wild in the burial ground.

This is a city of sleepwalkers, and elementary facts, such as the actual population, are given scant attention. No one knows how many people live in Juárez, though the current ballpark figure is closing in on two million. In 1994, 1.8 million poor Mexicans walked away from their dying earth and headed north. About 800,000 managed to cross into the United States. The remaining million slammed up against the fence in places like Juárez. Since then, this exodus has increased. Numbers are hard to come by but the feeling is not. Human flight from México has the American Border Patrol reeling. Juárez is part of the Mexican gulag, the place for the people no one wants.

Or Juárez is poor but full of soulful people. The factories pay very little but the workers are happy. There is crime and violence but it is localized and for the average person not of significance. Besides, American cities are notoriously dangerous. Juárez, if you wish, is like every other city on earth, terrible in spots but dynamic in the big picture. This belief is the hope of Homo sapiens, our way of living with things when they get unbearable. I've eaten in Juárez, drunk in Juárez, been happy in Juárez, and been sad in Juárez. I've done all these things in many cities. Like any twentieth-century man, I am largely a creature of these giant termitariums where my species now bunkers. But even with this background in urban manners and morals I am not sightless. Juárez has a distinct quality. It is the city where people may dream and fuck and drink and sing, but it is not the city where people hope.

For a while I've been asking North Americans a standard question when they tell me there is violence everywhere, when they tell me New York City is dan-

Opposite top: Miguel Perea. *Young women working in the maquiladora industry have lunch together.*
Opposite bottom: Julián Cardona. *At the end of their shift, workers at the Phillips #5 plant in the Gema industrial park board one of the hundreds of buses that carry personnel to and from the maquiladoras.*

gerous. I ask them: would you eat in a fine restaurant for free, a fabled venue with excellent food and a thousand seats, would you eat there if you knew that each and every night as you savored the paté and sipped a Mouton Rothschild, two out of the thousand diners would be slaughtered over their plates. This would be a kill rate of .2 of 1 percent, comparable to the impurity level in Ivory soap. When I ask this question, people look at me with discomfort and a touch of anger and quickly change the subject. I can sense in these moments that I have become an embarrassment. When they say that yes, the wages in places in Juárez are low but you must understand, they continue, these people can live on less because of lower prices and other factors always left unstated. To this thesis I make a simple and generous offer: I will take you to Juárez, deliver you across the bridge in a taxi, and then leave you on a street corner with 500 pennies. I will return in twenty-four hours and you can regale me with your good times.

The seventeen-year-old girl who has caught my attention was said to be found about a week after her disappearance in a desert tract embracing the city's southern edge, a place called the Lote Bravo. The girl worked six days a week in a foreign-owned factory making turn signals for automobiles. She took home the equivalent of $4 or $5 a day. In a photograph of her body handed to me by one of the photographers in the newspaper morgue, she is a crumpled figure on the desert floor surrounded by police who look officious and useless. The photographer told me that when she was found her panties were down around her ankles as the police circled her still form. At the time—late at night in the newspaper photo archive with the hum of fluorescent lights over my head and the bustle of staff rooting through the file cabinets—I took this statement at face value. At one time I'd done homicides for three years on an American newspaper, and the details of how human beings misuse and slaughter each other

Jaime Bailleres. *A raped and murdered woman found in Chamizal Park.*

had a familiar ring to me. But, of course, that moment in the morgue was early on, at a time when I still had a childlike faith in facts.

According to government officials, at least 150 girls disappeared in the city during 1995. The government offered that most ran off with boys, but some people doubted this explanation, and families would wander the Lote Bravo looking for loved ones and more and more bodies kept being found. The police then blamed an American serial killer and handily arrested a suspect. Girls continued to disappear. This particular girl's home address was in a neighborhood called Colonia Nueva Hermila. It is on no map I can find, but then hundreds of thousands of people here have no official existence. A taxi company queries its drivers by radio but no one knows this *colonia*. The bus drivers for the poor who prowl dirt lanes with broken-down machines think they have heard of it but cannot remember where it is. Finally, the fire department tries its hand at locating Colonia Nueva Hermila and comes up empty. But they say it is not a problem. If there is a fire there, they can find it by the smoke.

Jaime Bailleres has projected a beautiful black carved mask on the screen. The head is tilted and the face smooth with craftsmanship. The hair is long and black. It takes a moment for me to get past this beauty and realize the face is not a mask. She is a sixteen-year-old girl and they found her in the park by the Puente Libre linking Juárez to El Paso, Texas. The park on both sides of the Rio Grande is dedicated to friendship between the two nations. The skin has blackened in the sun, the face has contracted as it mummified. She was kidnapped, raped, murdered. Jaime explains that the newspaper refused to publish this photograph. The reason for this decision is very loud: the lips of the girl pull back, revealing her clean white teeth. Sound pours forth from her mouth. She is screaming and screaming and screaming.

"We don't think about the editors," Jaime snaps. "We don't give a damn about the editors. We can educate people. To look. To watch. We work in a jungle."

Jaime Murrieta. *Parents whose daughters (all maquiladora workers) have been murdered plead for justice and criticize the authorities for not protecting the women of Cd. Juárez.*

DE LAS SRITAS:
SILVIA. E. RIVERA
ORRES·ANGELICA MARQUES
JUSTICIA

The face floats on the screen as music purrs through the stereo speakers. No one will ever publish this photograph, Jaime tells me. I start to argue with him but soon give up. I can't deny one jolting quality of the image: it is deafening.

It is after midnight when Jaime's photo show breaks up and I head downtown. A wind whips across Juárez. The city often sprawls under moving walls of dust since so little of it is paved. The whores are out, sixteen-, seventeen-, and eighteen-year-olds. There is no way to tell if they are full-time prostitutes or factory workers making an extra buck. The peso has lost another chunk of its value in the last day or so.

"How much?" I ask.

She leans into the car window and says the equivalent of fourteen dollars. Of course, that includes the room.

"How long?" I ask.

"How long can you resist me?" she asks with a laugh.

There are ways to measure the deep movements of an economy that are more accurate and timely than the bond market and this girl with her mask of thick makeup is one of them.

"Juárez," photographer Julián Cardona explains, "is a sandwich. The bread is the First World and the Third World. We are the baloney." Julián, about thirty, is a tall, long-legged, thin man with a deep voice. On the street they call him El Compás, The Compass. He laughs easily and always seems to be watching. One night at the newspaper as I plowed through a thick stack of negatives from the Lote Bravo, he watched me like a hanging judge. Finally, I plucked a negative of a cop holding up the shoe of a dead girl found out in the desert. Cardona looked at it and for the first time allowed himself a small smile. "This is a good image," he said, almost with relief. I had passed, or at least gotten a stay of execution.

Like all the shooters in Juárez, Julián is keenly aware of the seasons. Following the harvest in November and December, there is a good crop of drug murders as the merchandise moves north and accounts are set-

tled. Then around Christmas and New Year's people hang themselves. The first few months of the new year bring fires and gas explosions as the poor try to stay warm. Spring means battles between neighborhoods (or colonias) over ground for building shacks, and outbreaks of disease in a city largely lacking sewage treatment. Summer brings water problems to a head (in theory, Juárez will run completely out of water within five years unless something is done), more disease, and batches of murders by the street gangs. The cool days of fall open a new season of battles between colonias, and then with the holidays the photographers return to drug killings and Christmas suicides. People seldom smile in Juárez. A reporter from México City took a look around and said, "This is a blue city." Or as Manuel Sáenz, a photographer on the morning paper, puts it, "Anything can happen here at any time. It can blow at any second." That is the inside of the sandwich.

Julián, like many of the street shooters in Juárez, sees his work as a mission. Juárez is the sixth-largest city in México and is historically famous for vice and violence. Since the end of World War I, it has been a place that draws Americans for women and dope. In 1995, crime probably increased about 30 percent (given crooked cops and crooked government, solid numbers are hard to come by), a new world record it shared with México City. What is happening in the city is often dismissed by simply saying that many cities are violent, gangs occur in the United States also, strife and dislocation are just the normal growing pains of a society industrializing, and so forth. All of these statements make sense except that they are polite lies. They are the governmental and intellectual version of that typical American sign off on unseemly experiences: shit happens. What these various shrugs do is admit the object—the body, the knife, the pollution, the poverty, the crime—and at the same time deny or refuse to admit the verb or the subject. In other words, things happen but we will not state who makes them happen or why they happen.

The photographers of Juárez believe that their work will state the truth. They say their cameras are

Above: Julián Cardona. *Every Friday and Saturday night, U.S. teenagers invade Cd. Juárez's Avenida Juárez, where, unlike in El Paso, they can drink alcoholic beverages, go to discos, and party until five or six in the morning.*

more deadly than AK-47s. We tend to favor mystical explanations for crime (that fabled gene that makes people evil, the complicated relations between a child and a parent, the muddling that occurs in the cortex when people take dope, the collapse in simple Biblical teachings imbibed around the family hearth, and so forth). We will consider any cause of murder and rape and robbery and general mayhem—except lack of work and lack of money. Any statement that implies that if you treat people like garbage they tend to behave badly is quickly dismissed as simplistic, the ultimate term for stupidity in our times.

Because if the problem is about money and work, nothing can change unless we change, and we are not up for such toil, and neither, apparently, is our beloved inner child.

Julián Cardona is on his way home at 7 A.M. after twelve hours of prowling the blood of the city's night. He catches a glimpse of a small crowd out of the corner of his sleepy eyes and pulls over. The man has been stabbed thirty times, and the arms are frozen in rigor mortis. A police technician is crouched over the chest photographing forensic evidence. Julián snaps off a few frames.

In any field that matters, the young devour the old. It is no different in the centuries-old community of Juárez, where Alfredo Carrillo storms through the work of earlier masters with a hungry and predatory

eye. Manuel Alvarez Bravo, the great Mexican photographer, is now ninety-five and settled into a routine, established a decade or so ago, of primarily aiming his camera at naked women and trees. But his life's work is a haunting montage of the surreal plucked from everyday Mexican life—a dead striker, men eating at a cheap taco stand, a woman holding a glass beside her abundant breasts. For years, I have loved Alvarez Bravo's work and used to marvel at his relative lack of fame in the United States. Now I sit in Juárez having a drink with Alfredo as he hacks away at the great man's work, a gringo defending a Mexican master from a young wolf. Alfredo has quick eyes, a short but muscular body, and he always seems both relaxed and coiled. Alvarez Bravo's decades of shots become playing cards in our discussion, and Alfredo's eyes announce to me that he was put on earth to shred and surpass the old man's musings. He will take his camera into the streets and show us. Thank God for this carnage between generations.

I'm sure a young Alvarez Bravo once fingered his camera in much the same way, as a weapon for dreamed-of assaults upon a dumb and uncaring world. Alfredo has some of his black-and-white prints on the table next to our drinks and he autographs

them for me as promissory notes against that future he will make with his camera. One is of a street urchin, a very young girl, looking sadly up at the driver of a car. The shot was snapped at the very second that her begging for coins was met with a firm no. I stare at her stringy hair and broken eyes.

Snapshots make Juárez stand still. You can run from photographs but you can't really hide. This seems to keep the photographers going. A shooter is desperate to get the shot of a man who has cut off his genitals in a moment of serious depression. But by the time the photographer arrives, the mutilated man is in the ambulance and the doors are closed. So the shooter pops open the back doors and clambers in. The man lying there is in shock, his crotch a pool of gore. He raises his head just as the photographer leans forward and goes click. The photographer is no fool and he knows this photograph will never be printed. He just wants it all.

His name is Jaime Murrieta and he is in his mid-thirties. He never turns off his police scanner. He beats the cops to many crime scenes and once got a medal from the city for rescuing someone from a blaze when he arrived ahead of the firemen. He has photographed over 500 murders. Once he crouched over the bloated body of a girl raped and murdered. The corpse exploded. He sighs when he thinks of the Pentax he used. It never worked again. Now we are in a car moving through downtown Juárez at about sixty miles an hour. The streets are clogged with people and we miss hitting them by inches. I feel like I am in a long dolly shot from an Indiana Jones sequence. It is seven minutes after five in the afternoon and Murrieta has just heard of a shooting in Colonia Juárez, down near the river. He is exploding with sheer joy. "I love violence," he tells me.

The other night around eleven, two women and a twelve-year-old girl drove a Dodge Ram Charger down the streets of Juárez. All three were shot in the head with a .45, a caliber favored by the federal police. Murrieta got some shots of them slumped in their car seats. This morning he covered the funeral and was beaten by the relatives, who were narco-traficantes. He showed me the contacts of the bereaved a few minutes before the murder call came over the scanner. He is tough on machines and burns out his clunkers in three or four months. No matter, he must keep changing vehicles anyway so that the gangs don't recognize what he is driving. Recently, seven rounds ripped through his car and somehow missed him. He has been beaten by the police several times and faced bullets and knives. Street shooters in Juárez face a critical audience of cops, gang members, and drug dealers. Murrieta has a photograph of his swollen face after one such beating. He smiles as he displays it to me.

"Yes, I am afraid," he admits. "But I love my work. I am on a mission and everything has its risk. God helps me." He has this dream of his death. Someone is coming at him with a gun or a knife and there is nowhere to run. As they fire at him or shove in the blade, he raises his camera and gets the ultimate murder photograph. "I will die happy," he insists. At the moment, he's been warned that a contract killer is looking for him. He is not that easy to find. It has taken me days to rendezvous with him since he moves ceaselessly through the night, comes and goes from the newspaper without warning, and seems to live more in his car than under any other roof.

In Colonia Juárez, the body we have come to see sprawls in front of the doorway of a corner grocery store. Three rounds from a .38 Special went through the head, five tore up the chest. That was twelve minutes ago. Francisco Javier Hernandez was also known as El Pelón, Baldy. According to optimistic police figures, he is murder number 250 this year in Juárez.

Opposite: Alfredo Carrillo. *The sense of violence, of loss of innocence, permeates Cd. Juárez.*
Below: Jaime Murrieta. *One of the bloodier narco executions in Cd. Juárez.*

At 5 P.M. he was twenty years old. He was a junkie, and he also sold drugs. He belonged to the pandilla called K-13, a group noted for its arsenal of guns. A crowd of his fellow gang members stands silently in the street.

Jaime Murrieta leaps out of the car and hits the street running. At first the police keep him back, but then I offer the captain a pack of Lucky Strike cigarettes and the officer's face brightens. I light one for him—there are these moments when I love México. Jaime scurries into the crime scene as the captain and I savor a smoke. His face is absolutely serene as he crouches over the body. Hernandez wears trousers and boots but his coat is almost off and the wound in the chest is visible in the good light that all photographers pray for. A pool of brilliant red blood frames his head like a halo. The storefront is pure white with a painting of Mickey Mouse. A sign over the doorway says "SIEMPRE COKE." Across the street is a pink house where drugs are sold. A fat girl smiles at the body. Her T-shirt says "KISS ME, I'M YOURS." There was a killing at this very corner four months ago.

At least a hundred people now stand in the street. The guys have empty faces and arms covered with tattoos. They make the sign of the cross with the briefest gesture. Two girls of about fifteen look at El Pelón. One holds a baby a few months old. They also belong to K-13. The killers are members of Los Harpys and the police are off at the moment to bag a few as suspects. The police station is nearby. Buses full of workers creep past the intersection and passengers stand and crane their heads out the windows to get a better view. No one seems upset.

El Pelón's mother stands a few feet from his corpse. Her hair is gray and she cradles her face with her hands. She is angry at her son. Only a week before, Los Harpys tried to kill him, and still he took no precautions. "This happened," she says, "because he is a *pendejo*, a sucker."

A twelve-year-old girl strolls down the sidewalk, drawn by the possibility of excitement. She has dyed red hair and the smooth and serene face of a child. She pushes through the crowd and sees the body. It is her brother. The contours of her face disintegrate as if she were a plate-glass window through which a rock has suddenly been hurled. She silently weeps and then the deep moans of a wounded animal rumble out of her small body. Two girls take her arms and hold her up as she slumps toward the ground.

Murrieta stops shooting. He is out of rationed film.

Jaime Bailleres has magically appeared at this murder scene and we start talking about the risk of this kind of work. He remembers covering one public protest when suddenly some cars pulled up and guys jumped out shooting. He did not move, he just kept clicking his camera like a robot. Later that night as he lay by his wife in bed, he began to shake and his mind filled with one thought: I could have been killed today.

Murrieta is a legend among the other street shooters. They love to tell a story about him. He is in bed with a woman and his police scanner is on. Murrieta is just about to climax when he hears a murder report crackle on the radio. He gets up and starts to dress.

The woman asks, "What are you doing?"

"I must go," he answers, "it is an obligation."

"You are not going to finish?"

"No."

The season of the winds has come, and in the squatter communities studding Juárez, the ground hangs brown in the sky and you chew it constantly. Jaime Bailleres has run out of hope as this wind pounds the city. Normally he is a boisterous, outsized personality, the hands moving, the smile flashing on and off, the voice rocketing along wild with excitement and laughter. He is the man whose manner says, I am willing. He moves with a language that shouts, What the hell. Now he sits in his apartment as the wind pounds the city and tells me how it is hopeless, how his job is fucked, photography is fucked, everything is fucked, and what has fucked it is the lack of money. There is no money, the Mexican economy continues to die around him, and he has the wife and the child and what kind of life is this?

I sit with him for an hour or two as he wades in a swamp of disgust and anger and gloom. For months,

I have been trying to buy a print from him and he has always put me off. Now he asks, How come you refuse to buy a photo from me?

I roll with the punch and write him a check. Somehow this makes the wind in the room die down and the pressure lift. I tell him I'll hang the image on the wall so that when I work I will look at it.

For months afterward, he asks me where I have hung the print. And for months I tell him I look at the photograph every single day when I sit down to work, and then he will smile quietly.

In a simple sense the photographs come from cameras, but there is a deeper point of origin. The floor under the gore of Juárez is an economy of factories owned by foreigners, mainly Americans. I keep having a repetitive experience when I talk with Americans about the foreign-owned factories in Juárez. I'll tell them the wages, the equivalent of $3, $4 or $5 a day, and they'll nod knowingly, and then a few minutes later, I will realize they have unconsciously translated this daily rate into an hourly rate. When I practically drill the actual wages into people, they naturally counter by saying the cost of living is much cheaper in México. This is not true. Along the border, Mexican prices run on average 85 to 90 percent of U.S. prices. What is happening in México betrays our notion of progress, and for that reason we face down these facts, and others, by insisting that each ugly little statistic is an exception or temporary or untrue. For example, in the past two years wages in the maquiladoras have risen 50 percent. Well and good. But inflation in that period is well over 100 percent.

Juárez is a museum of the history of the fabled New World Order, in which capital moves easily and labor is trapped by borders. Antonio Bermúdez and his son-in-law René Mascareñas were early boosters of the city's industrial growth—Mascareñas winding up in a 16,000-square-foot house stuffed with his collection of cannons, swords, pikes, and battle banners. Now their legacy studs the city. There are at least 325 foreign-owned factories in Juárez, the

Above: Gabriel Cardona. *A lanchero takes Mexicans in search of better opportunities across the Rio Grande to El Paso.*
Pages 78–79: Jaime Bailleres. *Ambassadors from around the world visit the Thomson maquiladora in Cd. Juárez, where a technical manager explains certain aspects of the assembly line.*

highest concentration in all of México, and they employ over 175,000 workers. All of these industrial areas are built on land allegedly stolen by the city's leading families. The factory concept, called the twin-plant system (or, in Spanish, maquiladoras), was created by the U.S. and México in 1965 so that Americans could exploit cheap Mexican labor without paying high Mexican tariffs. Although the products that come from the factories are counted as Mexican exports (and thus figured into the Gross Domestic Product), nothing is actually made here. All the parts are shipped to México from the United States and the workers assemble them and then ship them back. Economists figure that only 2 percent of "material inputs used in *maquila* production come from Mexican suppliers."

Juárez is in your home when you turn on the microwave, watch television, take in an old film on the VCR, slide into a new pair of blue jeans, listen to the radio, make toast in the kitchen, enjoy your kid playing with that new toy truck. Old and familiar names turn up, like RCA, Westinghouse, Sunbeam, General Electric, Motorola, Tonka. Two or three thousand American managers commute back and forth from El Paso each day. Originally, maquilas were restricted to within twenty kilometers of the border. Gradually, in the 1980s, this regulation loos-

ened, and then with the passage of NAFTA in late 1993, all of México became the potential host for maquiladoras. For years the twin plants of the border had slowly sputtered along. Then, with the collapse of México's economy in 1982, a bonanza occurred: suddenly wages were lower here than in the mills of Southeast Asia, and a boom began in the maquila industry.

Politicians and economists speculate about a global economy fueled by free trade. Their speculations are not necessary. In Juárez the future is over thirty years old, and there are no questions about its nature that cannot be answered in this city. The inside of the sandwich can be touched, measured, photographed, and tasted by all. As one Mexican friend told me, "I live in a laboratory."

The maquilas have caused millions of poor people to move to the border. In 1900, maybe 100,000 people lived along the border. Now the number is at least twelve million and rising. Most of the workers are women and most of the women are young. By a person's late twenties or early thirties, the body slows and cannot keep up the pace of the work. Then, like any used-up thing, the people are junked. Turnover in the maquilas runs anywhere from 50 to 150 percent a year. In Tijuana, for example, where much of the world's television-production industry is now based, it bangs along at 8 percent a month. It is common for workers in Juárez to leave for work at 4 A.M. and spend one or two hours navigating the dark city to their jobs. Sometimes they wind up in the Lote Bravo. The companies do offer some bus rides along certain routes. Also, they carefully screen the girls to make sure they are not pregnant: workers at one plant complain of a company rule that new female hires present bloody tampons for three

consecutive months. The work week is generally six days, forty-eight hours. After work some of the girls go downtown to sell their bodies for money or food or drinks. Friday night is especially noted for this marketing. The street shooters all tell me, "You want fucking? We'll go there Friday night and you'll get fucking." At least 40 percent of the Mexican labor force now lives off the underground economy, which means they stand in the street and try to sell things, anything, including themselves. Some feel this number is too low. The World Bank recently reported that 75 percent of all Mexicans live below the poverty line.

Workers who lose their jobs receive essentially no benefits beyond severance pay. México has no safety net. Real unions simply do not exist and anyone trying to organize one is fired. Or murdered. A good example of labor's rights in México is the strike in a Ford plant near México City in 1987. The conflict was triggered by the company's shutdown of the 5,000-man facility. Ford declared the old contract junk and cut a deal with the official government union, CTM, which slashed wages 50 percent and got rid of seniority. After that, only 3,800 of the original workers were rehired. When an effort was made to form an independent union, things got tough. CTM thugs fired on workers, wounding nine and killing one. When the workers seized the plant, Ford asked then-President Carlos Salinas to send in the cops, and he did. Finally, there was an election to vote for the CTM union or an independent union. Two thousand cops surrounded Ford during the balloting—each worker had to appear on television and announce his vote. CTM won and workers who wanted to keep their jobs had to sign a statement in which they confessed that their brief interest in their own union was "due to confusion or lack of reflection." Though recent Mexican political elections have displayed hopeful signs of less fraud, this reform has yet to reach the factory floors.

Real wages have been falling since the '70s. And since the wages are just a hair above the starvation level, the maquilas contribute practically nothing toward forging a consumer society. Of course, as maquiladora owners and managers point out, if wages are raised, the factories will move to other countries with a cheaper labor force. It is almost impossible to get ahead working in maquilas.

Industry is thriving. Half a million cargo-laden trucks move from Juárez to El Paso each year. Boxcars of products rumble over the railroad bridge. New industrial parks are opening up. Labor is functionally limitless, as tens of thousands of poverty-stricken people pour into the city each year. The hundreds of maquiladoras in Juárez get an annual tax bill from the city. Until 1995, this bill was zero— but that year the maquiladoras voluntarily donated the equivalent of $1 million to the city (at the time about $2,857 apiece). In January of 1996, Juárez became the first municipality in México to institute a tax on the maquiladoras. The rate is .5 to 1 percent of the total payroll per month. It remains to be seen how much of this tax will ever actually be collected. There are few environmental controls on the maquiladoras and little enforcement of those that do exist. El Paso/Juárez is one of the most polluted spots in North America. And yet it is a success story. In Juárez the economic growth in 1993 was 2 percent, in 1994 it was pegged at 6 percent, and in 1995 it registered 12 percent. According to Lucinda Vargas, the U.S. Federal Reserve economist who tracks México's economy, Juárez is a "mature" economy. Apparently, this is as good as it gets.

The street shooters of Juárez are seldom allowed to take photographs inside the factories. Yet it is a challenge to take a photograph of anything in Juárez without capturing the consequences of the maquiladoras. With the passage of NAFTA, narcotraficantes began buying maquiladoras in Juárez. They did not want to miss out on the advantages of free trade.

The workers in the maquiladoras have created a new school of architecture that to date has not been seriously studied by scholars. They build homes out of odd materials—cardboard, old tires, pallets stolen from loading docks. The structures are held together with nails driven through bottle caps—a cheap bolt. Earth tones predominate. The designs flow unhampered by building codes. No school of aesthetics scolds, no committee votes, no zoning oppresses. Like the fabled Pilgrims, the people of the shantytowns have largely escaped the notice of the rulers and have been left to their own devices. The only limit is the energy to scavenge a world. A woman sweeps a dirt yard while a plant glows by the door in a coffee can. Washed clothes dry on barbed wire. There is something primal about such housing and something deeply satisfying about its existence. It is a salsa version of the impulse behind the New England village, reborn in a garbage dump.

Electricity is stolen from power lines. Jaime Bailleres took photos of a man up a power pole illegally clamping into a high-voltage line. The man was inept: as Bailleres took his picture, the man was electrocuted. Water is more difficult to acquire, and in many of the shanty communities of Juárez it must be bought off trucks. Land for housing is also scarce, and is often stolen by the poor.

Gabriel Cardona, another Juárez photographer, has recorded a land invasion. It begins when a woman notices that her portrait of Christ is weeping. Soon, her colonia has built a shrine out of scavenged wood and the painting is surrounded by hundreds of votive candles. This miraculous painting inspires the local people to invade some vacant land and throw up huts. The next photo is of a man returning from work in a maquiladora to his home. It has been bulldozed by the police, and he stares at his bed and a bucket and a few other items piled up on the scraped earth.

Above and right: Jaime Bailleres. *Many Cd. Juárez residents cannot afford electrical connections for their homes. Jaime Ramírez Sánchez accidentally electrocuted himself while trying to steal electricity.*
Below: Manuel Sáenz. *Each winter Cd. Juárez sees an epidemic of deaths from carbon monoxide poisoning because of faulty or makeshift heaters.*

Above: Jaime Bailleres. *In mid-1994, a family living in Colonia México 68 announced that their image of the Sacred Heart was bleeding. For the family and their neighbors, it was a miracle. Many gathered around while a matachín (folk dancer) went into a trance. Tourists from the United States soon began to arrive as well. Left: Julián Cardona. On 6 January 1997, Tarahumara Indians celebrating El Dia de Reyes, one of three important annual Tarahumara festivities, dance and drink their traditional corn-derived liquor, Tesgüino, while snow begins to fall.*

(Snow also falls inside the church, which is built out of maquiladora waste.)
Above: Gabriel Cardona.
Easter Mass, organized by the Catholic Church in Cd. Juárez.
Right: Julián Cardona.
Bishop Renato Ascencio León of Cd. Juárez arriving at the city's airport. Behind him is the former bishop of Cd. Juárez, Juan Sandoval Iñiguez, who now serves as the archbishop of Guadalajara, his predecessor there having been assassinated, allegedly by narcotraficantes.
Pages 86–87: Aurelio Suárez Núñez. *Catholics in Cd. Juárez unite for an Easter celebration.*

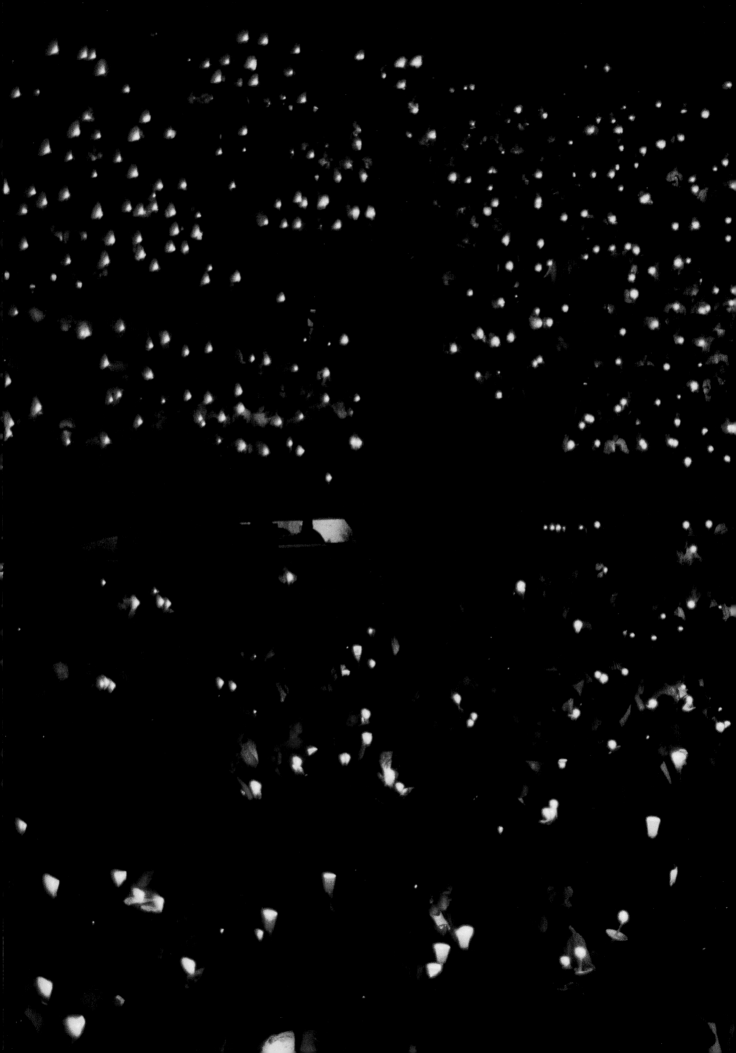

The two daily newspapers in El Paso, that city of half a million or more that squats thirty feet from Juárez, can go days without a single story about the one to two million people living in poverty right before everyone's eyes. A single killing sums up this attitude. Someone slaughtered a retired Juárez cop, José Refugio Ruvalcaba, and two of his sons. Then they tied them with yellow rope and made a yellow bow. Then they put them in the trunk of the car, drove to the midpoint of a bridge between El Paso and Juárez, and abandoned the vehicle so that it straddled the boundary line. The plan worked. Neither country would accept the responsibility for investigating what had happened.

Manny Sáenz cannot trust and he knows this fact and admits this fact. For months, I have been trying to borrow prints and slides from the photographers to show magazine editors in New York. Jaime Bailleres, in his ebullient way, holds a kind of soliloquy with himself in the corner of a room as we all meet, and then announces with the gravity of an oracle that he will trust me. Alfredo Carrillo soon follows suit, and then Julián Cardona. Gabriel Cardona waffles and then succumbs to a degree. But Manny sits there tense and torn and finally tells me he wants to trust, he really wants to trust. But he cannot trust. It is not in him. He shrugs at this fact as if it were a matter of natural law that neither of us can do much about. Finally, against his will and better judgment, he entrusts me with his best shots.

Months later I am in Juárez when I bump into him. He is coming out of the squatter hell of Anapra and is beaming with excitement. Look, he explains, the police are very near to a solution, they are going to arrest the men who have been killing the girls, some strange cabal of murderers. He trusts this information absolutely, his belief bears not the slightest shadow of doubt. This happens periodically in a world like Juárez, a place of cowed newspapers, radio, and television, a ground of crooked government and police either hapless or hideous. No one, it seems, can sustain the reality. And so from time to time,

Mexicans suddenly shift in mid-sentence and tell you with horror of a crooked cop or politician who lies or steals as if they had discovered some unique and frightening mutant. Manny Sáenz, who cannot trust, stands in the midday sun and tells me the police are very close to cracking the case, justice is at hand.

I'm drinking with Julián Cardona toward midnight in the district of Juárez where the workers of the maquilas gather on a Saturday night to dream away their dead-end lives. The disco is huge and holds maybe 800 or 1,000 kids all dressed in their very best clothes and drinking as if money were no object and tomorrow had no power over their minds. Buckets of long-necks sit on the tables and the girls in T-shirts and see-through blouses have a glazed look as the alcohol or other solaces kick in. The boys stare yearningly yet maintain passive faces. The crowd is squandering much of its paltry wages on a night of revels. Some of the factory girls are hooking on the side and the waiters offer help for any type or age desired. The sound is loud, the room dark, and the odors of beer, urine, smoke, and perfume lie like a paste on the crowd.

For five years Julián worked in a maquiladora, and the kids kicking back strike fond memories in him.

"I was a fool," he allows of his years in the factory, "but a happy fool."

And surely this is true, just as it is true for some in brothels, skid rows, or wars. I have even known those who were happy in high school. But like many such activities, what is more telling is how few are willing to return to them once they escape into the dream we call a future.

There is a hesitation when the street shooters of Juárez mention La Pantera, The Panther. Once he was one of them, a fellow photographer on the newspaper. Then he took up the video camera and went to work for a television station. But it is his dedication to his work that gives the street shooters pause. They feel he has gone too far, that living as he does he cannot survive. He has raised the stakes.

Rafael Cota, better known as La Pantera, worked twelve hours a day, seven days a week, for six years. Recently, he's cut back to a six-day week. He works only at night and his name comes in part from his eerie ability to get to the murders before the police, in part from his fantasy that he has feline moves and a touch of Peter Sellers' Inspector Clouseau about his wanderings. Sometimes he videotapes things the police do not wish to have publicized. He is in his thirties and has a quiet and reserved manner. His camera has stared at close to 1,000 murders. Five times the police have beaten him and destroyed his equipment. Narcotraficantes also look at him with disfavor. La Pantera wears a bulletproof vest. He is said to have one of the highest-rated television programs in the city—a program on which his face has never appeared.

"It's exciting," he tells me, "it is the life of the problems of this city." His day begins with darkness and

Jaime Bailleres. City police and federales got into a fight when police patrolling a middle-class neighborhood mistook machine-gun-bearing federales in a car for narcotraficantes. The two police forces almost began shooting at each other. The federales claimed they were on their way to investigate a possible drug deal, and said the police interference had forced them to abort their mission. In Cd. Juárez, it is often difficult to distinguish between federales and narcotraficantes.

ends with light, and in between he roams alone in an old black pickup truck, a police scanner always plugged into his left ear. He shoots murders, car accidents, suicides, gang fights, all the violence of the night hours.

For several years he rode with an assistant and then they fell in love and married. She continued riding with him, and one night when she was nine months pregnant, the labor pains came, and La Pantera made a brief pit stop at the hospital so that their daughter could be born. For his long work week he is paid the equivalent of $100. He cannot live on this, so during the day he is a part-time fumigator. His daughter sometimes rides with him, "so she will learn reality."

La Pantera is convinced that if he shows people what their city is like, then they will change their city. That is why he left newspapers and still photography—television, he believed, would reach more people with more force. He worries about being killed but he cannot seem to stop. Being around him has the quality of visiting someone on death row. In your heart you know he can't possibly make it. Once he came upon Jaime Murrieta being beaten by narco-traficantes in a bar. La Pantera leaped in to help him and so they both were beaten almost to death. "I can keep doing this forever," he insists quietly to me. "This is a mission for justice." In his spare time, he and his wife work with the Red Cross. People come to him seeking help in finding the missing. He is a faceless legend. He refuses to appear on the screen because he does not want his personality to get in the way of the stories, the montages of horror that he constructs each and every night.

"I like to take the tragedies," he explains, "and make people feel them."

He is very proud of his work, and shelf after shelf in the station sags with the results of his nocturnal labor. He plucks a cassette and insists I watch. A man is beaten, blood coursing down his face, the soft voice of La Pantera narrating. Then comes a car wreck, a body bent and misshapen in the crumpled front seat. The camera pans to an empty bottle of rum on the ground. An ambulance arrives, the camera follows a gurney with the mutilated man rolling down a corridor. Suddenly, the face is very still, a hand moves into view and covers the corpse with a sheet. A cantina fills the frame, then an ambulance, a man knifed in a barroom fight. A few dozen *pandilleros* stand in the street, some injured from the gang fight.

La Pantera silently watches his tape with the calm pleasure of a connoisseur. He fast-forwards the tape and the people shouting and crying sound like cartoon characters. Then he slows the tape and the camera pans to a suicide. La Pantera punches the reverse button and runs this scene again and again. Forty frequencies from the scanner purr into his ear.

The man is quite young and wearing a bulky blue sweater. By his feet is a five-gallon bucket. The rope around his neck is tied to a small tree in a city park. His neck is bent but the rope is straight and taut. The camera frames the man and the tree, then zooms in to peruse his body, and quickly does a 180-degree pan around to his back. Then the camera zooms in again to one of his feet. It is touching the ground. During the hours he spent hanging here alone, his neck stretched, and now he is firmly planted on the earth again.

When I leave the station, La Pantera walks me out into the 2 A.M. street. He touches my shoulder and says, "Be careful. This is a very dangerous city. Do not stop at any stop signs. They will leap out and take the car." Of course, he departs also, since his work will not end until dawn.

Every morning around 7:45 A.M. La Pantera's program runs as a special eight-to-ten-minute part of the morning news. The segment is called "While You Were Sleeping."

We have drunk past the midnight hour and Gabriel Cardona is alive with the wine. He is a man of a sweet disposition and this shows in his images, which are infused with a kind of tenderness and affection, whatever the horror confronting his camera. I want to buy one print and we have tugged over this fact for hours. First, can he sell this print? He wavers and ducks and dances and then decides, yes, he can sell this print. A fire has swept a cardboard squatters' community and in the morning the place is burned flat, a charred landscape. In the foreground of his photograph, a two-year-old sits astride a burned-out bicycle, the round face turned toward the camera like a plate hosting a huge smile. The bike's tires are gone, the wheels themselves warped by the heat of the fire. A small dot of something is on the print, and when I ask Gabriel, he explains that it is a drop of sweat that fell on his lens while he was shooting.

Gabriel Cardona. *A two-year-old child playing in Colonia Universidad where just one day before a fire razed over sixty cardboard-and-wood homes. Like many of the colonias, this one has no electricity and no water or sewage system.*

Finally we agree on a price—he will not name one, I must divine the proper sum. We stand outside later in the night air and he asks, You are really going to hang my photograph on the wall? And I say yes. I tell him I need to look at the child's face in the ruined colonia and look at it often if I am going to keep facing the dawns.

In 1991, Nicholas Scheele, the head of Ford in México, said in admiration of the government's control, "But is there any other country in the world where the working class . . . took a hit in their pur-chasing power of in excess of 50 percent over an eight-year period and you didn't have a social revo-lution?" Maybe you get something you don't have to define as a revolution. There are over 450 gangs in Juárez. They, not the police, define the borders in the city. They, not the government, represent authority to the human beings in the colonias. They provide work selling narcotics. And they kill and steal all the time to protect what little sphere of power they have. They are not a progressive force, they are simply the force that grows when a society offers no progress. They have blossomed over the last three years as sev-eral factors made them inevitable: the slow decom-position of the Mexican government created a vacuum. The explosive growth of the drug industry created a livelihood. The mutilation of the main bul-wark of Mexican culture, the family, created a need.

For the women, the assembly plants are sometimes liberating since they are able to leave their homes and for the first time in their lives have their own money. But there is a price. The collapse of marriages and of families increases.

México had to create one million jobs a year for young people entering the economy. Instead, the country in 1995 lost at least one to two million jobs. And most important, the fabled pull of the border brought hordes of almost neolithic peasant families to a city where their past skills were worthless. In Juárez you find Stone Age parents staring helplessly at Computer Age children. Nothing the adults know or can provide has much value here, and the fabric that has held families and México together tears right before your eyes. You can actually hear the tearing. I'll be standing at a murder scene, the shooters will be feeding on a fresh corpse, and as I make notes I can hear the gang kids murmuring about me. When I look up I see very hard eyes and I know everyone but me is packing. There is nothing to be done about this. I am like everyone else here, I simply go about my business as if death were not a few feet away dis-

guised as some twelve- or thirteen-year-old with a gun and with eyes older than I can ever hope to be.

This new world makes stabs at beauty. Juárez historically is a cultural cauldron where folk México confronts and fabricates life out of the high technology of its American neighbor. In the 1940s, *pachuco* culture, with its zoot suits, exploded out of Juárez. Black-velvet painting also started here. The pandillas, like many U.S. gangs, at first spray-painted signs on walls, then started doing full-figure paintings. Otto Campbell, a noted Juárez artist, became interested in their work and offered to teach them. And so he did.

In the early '90s, they seized a wall in downtown Juárez and created a massive, block-long mural. With its background blood red, the mural featured historical figures like those painted by Diego Rivera and José Clemente Orozco in the 1920s. But with a difference. Intermingled with historical personages were modern *cholos* in gang dress and the entire work pivoted on the central figure of La Catrina. She was burned into the consciousness of México by a turn-of-the-century artist named José Guadalupe Posada, who produced daily comments on current events using drawings of skeletons. La Catrina is the woman of wealth with the large-brimmed hat, the symbol of vanity and greed. In the mural created by the pandilleros, La Catrina had her famous hat, her smiling skull, and hints of her bony torso. But she was in this rendering also of the flesh, and wore black stockings and a garter belt. She was the whore. The mural became famous in Juárez and flamed from the formerly blank wall of BancaPromex. But apparently it did not conform to the company's image or to the government's desires, and so one night a crew surreptitiously painted it out. The family who owns the bank building also has the Coca-Cola bottling con-

cession in Juárez. Where the mural once was, it currently reads: "COCA-COLA ES LA CHISPA: NO ANUNCIAR" (Coca-Cola is the sparkle: Post no bills).

The pandilleros moved on to another mural project. Julián Cardona holds a large photograph of this work. It is an image of the Puente Negro, the black railroad bridge linking El Paso and Juárez. The view is from the Mexican side. American officials have erected massive sliding doors on the bridge to block people from crossing, and the pandilleros have painted these doors in the style of the old master Mexican muralists. Peasants are marching along the bottom of the mural. Above them are the girders and machines of modern industrial life and blood is spilling from this future.

In the photograph, taken by Jaime Bailleres, the doors are being closed after the train enters the U.S. from México. The locomotive is blue and huge and stares out like a cyclops with its white beam. It looks like the train will move forward and kill the peasants any second.

Cardona stabs at the photograph and tells me, "This is a great image. The hands that can make this

Opposite: Lucio Soria Espino. *Tarahumara Indians wait by the cathedral in Cd. Juárez for their Spanish classes to begin.*
Below: Manuel Sáenz. *Painted by young* cholos *from the various colonias, this mural expressing the ancient culture of México is part of an antigraffiti campaign.*
Pages 94–95: Jaime Bailleres. *The border gate on the Puente Negro, with a mural painted by Mexican cholos and gang members and showing the enslavement of Mexicans, is closed after a train leaves México for the United States.*

painting, those hands kill almost 150 people in this city every year." And then he sighs. Half of this mural has now been removed.

Above: Miguel Perea. *A farmer in the Ejido Zaragoza* (ejido *refers to communal property*) *cleaning corn.*
Opposite: Lucio Soria Espino. *During this probably drug-related execution, the victim was tortured before being murdered.*

After a while, after several months, things in Juárez begin to haunt me. I try to put my finger on what exactly is bothering me. I tell myself it is not simply the poverty—I remember being in delta shacks in the segregated Mississippi of the '60s and people living almost like animals deep within the bosom of my own country. When I lived with these people for weeks and weeks, I consumed what they ate—wild greens picked by the road and fried in grease, bootleg liquor made in the thickets by the river. I can also remember working on the west side of Chicago in districts that had the look and feel of Berlin in the summer of 1945 after a couple of years of American

carpet-bombing. But Juárez is different in a way that tables of wages and economic studies cannot capture. Finally, I can say what I have sensed for months: in Juárez you cannot sustain hope.

The women are standing outside the door of the American-owned maquiladora. It is payday and they want to grab their men before they drink up their wages. Most of the women are pregnant. The rest are nursing. The scene occurs every week. Cameras, of course, are not allowed in this place except for promotional corporate pictures. I keep coming here to see a friend. He is a native of Juárez and one of the highly skilled few who make good money in a maquiladora—in his case the equivalent of about $100 a week, or five grand a year. He is my guide to the dangerous barrios because he is short and dark and one of them.

Nearby, almost in the shadow of the maquiladora, sprawls a colonia. The huts are cardboard and wooden pallets, the electricity pirated, the water trucked in, the streets dust. My friend takes me into this CDP (Committee for popular defense, an early effort to organize the poor) barrio, one of at least twenty-six in Juárez. The police are afraid to enter CDP settlements. The residents work in maquilas and sell drugs, guns, and cars stolen from the U.S. They also make bricks. It is dusk and they have fired up their kilns using tires for fuel. Black tongues of thick smoke lick the shacks. The main dirt lane of the colonia is blocked by a circle of people sitting on buckets. They are having a community meeting. This is the order in the new world.

There are other hints of the emerging order. Jaime Bailleres is in a nightclub and at his editor's insistence he takes a picture of a beautiful woman for the newspaper's lifestyle section. A man at another table is accidentally included in the frame. Suddenly, two bodyguards lay their hands on Bailleres. They do not want this picture published, understand? He wonders, Is this man now stored somewhere in his camera Amado Carrillo? But this thought is dangerous. When I mention the name out loud at the bar, he looks around quickly to see if anyone has overheard. His eyes for a few seconds show true panic. Jaime is hardly a coward but he is certainly not a fool like me.

The scenes are everywhere. The street shooters of Juárez spend very little time waiting. The banks are robbed between 8 A.M. and 3 P.M. The killings fill the nights—one Monday while I was there five went down in five consecutive hours. Or El Rata goes down in a drive-by shooting. The pandillas buy T-shirts emblazoned with his name to memorialize him, and the procession out of the dusty hills and shacks is led by gang members carrying his coffin. Manny Sáenz snaps the

picture. El Rata was twelve years old. Julián Cardona brings his camera up and captures children scavenging in a garbage dumpster. These matters can wear you down. The dry rot of government finishes the job.

Before one of the recent elections Bailleres found the reform (and opposition-party) governor of Chihuahua in a restaurant secretly meeting with the leaders of the nation's ruling party. The alarmed governor looked up at the camera and said, "I'm asking you as a personal favor not to take a picture." Bailleres fired off frame after frame. "That," he tells me with deep satisfaction, "is when I felt the power of photography." Of course, the governor made a call and the photos were never published.

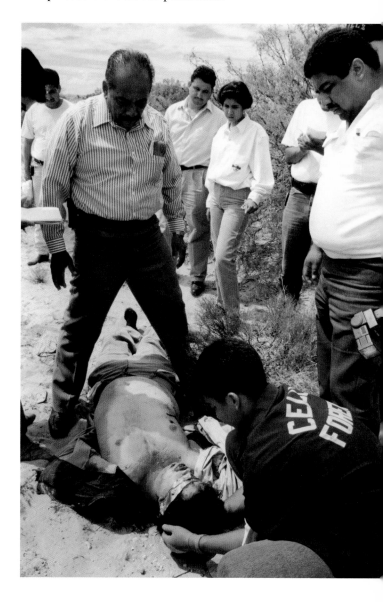

We all have a deep need to ignore Juárez. We write off what is going on by saying that it is something our grandparents or great-grandparents went through. But this will not work because the economy either shrinks (7 to 8 percent in 1995), or shows token growth of 3 percent in 1996 off a severely shrunken base. Besides, in México income distribution is not an idea. We are not looking at a temporary economic dip or even a depression. We are looking at long-term poverty, underemployment, and malnutrition. We tell ourselves that there are gangs and murders in American cities. This is true but it does not deal with the reality of Juárez. We are not talking about darkness on the edge of town or a bad neighborhood. We are talking about an entire city woven out of violence. We tell ourselves that jobs in the maquiladoras are better than nothing. But we ignore the low wages, high turnover, and shacks. Then there is a silent sentence that says . . . after all, they are Mexicans, not U.S. citizens. This kind of shrug brings to mind Descartes nailing his live family dog to a board and cutting it up to determine

if it had a soul. He believed animals could not feel pain.

We prefer not to discuss these facts. We would rather talk about free trade, the war on drugs, immigration reform. We insist we are in control. We are wrong. Neither our current policies nor any proposed policies offer the slightest hope of improvement in a place like Juárez. Our economic beliefs have had a three-decades-long run in that city. They are no longer theories, they are realities. Thirty feet from the United States we can see the future. We are brown and we are white, we are Mexicans and we are Americans, and we are all there, right this minute. We can dread this future but we cannot claim not to know what it will be like. The city looks like a Marxist cartoon, though it is hard to say whether it is the work of Karl or Groucho. No one wants to imagine what Juárez will be like if it doubles its industrial employment and goes from 325 factories to 650.

I'm standing by the Carranza sisters' cardboard shack in Anapra. They moved to the shantytown about ten months ago when three years of drought ended their lives in a village in Durango. A half-dozen murdered, mutilated, and raped girls have been found about a hundred yards from their shack and this frightens the teenage girls. Each morning they rise at 3:30 A.M., cook over bits of wood, and have some coffee. After a tortilla they are likely to walk out into the darkness with their few possessions (a pan, plate, knife, fork, spoon, and cooking oil) and bury them secretly in a hole—otherwise they will be stolen while they are gone. They are the lucky ones: five of them work in American-owned maquiladoras. The fifteen-year-old girl, the middle sibling, is a welder at 160 pesos a week (about $21 at current exchange rates). She spends two hours making various bus connections to arrive at work by 6 A.M. Public bus fare costs her 8 pesos a day. The sandy lot she shares with her brothers and sisters costs them the equivalent of about $6 a month in rent. Today the Carranza kids are fixing to plant eight pine seedlings. Tomorrow they begin their six-day weeks at American factories. The thought of shade and trees today, the fact of slave wages tomorrow.

They live at ground zero of the future. The United States begins fifty yards away, where the North Americans are constructing a steel wall to keep México at bay. In fact, the First World is so near that every few days a band of Anapra residents gather at around 8 P.M. and walk the short distance to the border, where an American railroad almost brushes against the fence. Then, as the bend in the tracks slows the train, they expertly crack open a dozen or more box cars, toss goods out to waiting hands and rush back into México, all in less than the two minutes it takes for cops to arrive. U.S. newspapers periodically print stories about these train robberies (hundreds in the last three years) and call the Carranzas' neighbors

Above right: Julián Cardona. *Children collect cans in order to earn some pesos toward supporting their families.*
Opposite: Julián Cardona. *"When we don't pay them their* cuota *(money paid to the police for protection), they remove us from our customers or arrest us," complains one of three small-time drug dealers who has just been arrested for possession of several grams of cocaine and a packet of marijuana.*

the new Jesse Jameses. But then Anaprans don't read U.S. newspapers or anything else. They just try to stay alive day by day.

Jaime Bailleres says, "Sometimes I feel like I am in Bosnia." He tells me a story to make sure my feeble gringo mind grasps what he means. The paper wanted a soft feature on the lives of the rich, so one Saturday a photographer and his editor strolled through an enclave of wealth looking for the right image. The photographer brought along his wife and two children. As a rabbit hopped across the lawn of a mansion, the camera came up. Suddenly, two bodyguards appeared with AK-47s and one said, "Give

Above: Jaime Bailleres. *The neighborhood of Misión de los Lagos (which contains neither mission nor lake) exemplifies how the richer residents of Cd. Juárez live. It is here that a photographer was beaten up when he tried to photograph a rabbit hopping across a mansion's lawn.*
Opposite top: Aurelio Suárez Núñez. *Burning homes in the Colonia Tierra y Libertad.*
Opposite bottom: Manuel Sáenz. *Although water is scarce and often absent altogether in the colonias, hosing each other down is a favorite summer pastime for children.*

me that fucking camera and film." They forced the photographer face down on the pavement with the automatic rifles at his head. Then, in front of his wife and children and editor, they beat him about his head, ribs, and genitals. Police stood nearby and watched. That is the end of the story.

None of this matters. It is all a detail or an exception or an illusion. The authorities announced back in November of 1995 that 520 people had disappeared in Juárez that year and "an important percentage of them are female adolescents." By March of 1996 the mothers of the missing were demonstrating and demanding justice. Then in April the police made a sweep of the red-light district, bagged 120 suspects, and the next day announced that they had solved the case. The authorities explained that the slaughter was the work of eight apparently gregarious sociopaths who hung out in a bar called Joe's Place. The next day the mothers of the accused protested the police torture of their sons. A year later girls were still disappearing and mothers were still protesting in front of the Juárez city hall. We'll probably never know exactly what has been going on. We will never know how many have actually disappeared, how many of the disappeared were murdered. We will discover killers from time to time and sometimes we will pounce on a serial killer—any city of two million probably has one on the job at any given moment. But we are unlikely to square off with the issue at hand—a city of poverty that has become a kind of killing machine.

The movies have not taught us how to deal with such a condition. Our films thrill us with terrors: a fiend operates, the citizens are afraid, and then they become angry. The chief—there is always a chief, we really must be tribal—calls in his best man, who is always unlucky in love, somewhat dissolute in his habits, and prone to breaking rules. He plunges into the city, which is always shown as a jungle of steel and concrete, and in about 120 minutes he locates the monster in our midst who is slaughtering our kind. There is a face-off that only the hero and the monster fully understand, and then the monster is slain and order returns. Sometimes the film ends with hints of another monster being hatched out in the community, a creature spawned by a deep biological drive for a sequel, but the mayhem we have witnessed, the gore we have bathed in, is still presented as singular, a contained thing to be wary of but unlikely to descend on our patio during any Saturday-afternoon barbecue. This is the basic movie running in our heads and we refer to it when anything slaps against our eyes and suggests that the violence may be general, not singular, deep-rooted, not ephemeral.

In July of 1996, one of the Juárez dailies published a front-page list of missing girls found dead in the Lote Bravo over the last year. The seventeen-year-old who had started my wandering was not on the list. It does not matter that I read of her disappearance in the same newspaper, or read the account of her body being found in the same newspaper, or examined photographs of her corpse in the Lote Bravo in the morgue of the same newspaper. Well, I can't find the neighborhood where she lived so I am hard-pressed to prove she ever existed. In fact, knowing something hardly matters. I am told that the seventeen-year-old never disappeared, then I am told yes, she disappeared but was not found. Then I am told she disappeared and was found, and yes, I did actually see that photograph in the newspaper morgue of the cops standing around her body, but that later the city's pathologist determined it was not really her body. So you see, we really can't know. What I now wonder is if we will ever really see.

The same day that the list appeared in the Juárez paper, an American drug conference took place at Fort Bliss on the edge of El Paso. The U.S. Attorney General, the Drug Czar, the head of the FBI, the head of Immigration, and other officials were there, and for days before, the newspapers bubbled with stories that the next candidate to make the FBI's most-wanted list would be one Amado Carrillo Fuentes. The night before, I was taken by a Mexican reporter to a mansion in El Paso surrounded by high walls and electronic gates and an array of electronic security-systems. We sat outside and looked at the mansion's bristling efforts at privacy. I was told the building belonged to a family with serious organized-crime connections and that for the past week Amado Carrillo Fuentes had been staying there to get some peace amid the hubbub. Perhaps he caught the drug conference on television—CNN was supposed to broadcast some of it live. I couldn't prove Carrillo was inside the mansion, I couldn't do that if I entered and shackled him. No one really knew what he looked like. I did call up someone I knew in the U.S. drug-enforcement world and ran my evening by him and told him of squatting outside of Carrillo's alleged hideaway in El Paso. He listened carefully and then said, "It doesn't surprise me a bit." Well, no matter. I've gone native.

I come and go in Juárez and then return to a different world where things still seem to work, payday comes now and then, and over a good dinner what I know and have seen can be buried. Alive. After all, I would rather smile and feel the sun against my face than think about Juárez, or all the other places like Juárez that are growing quietly like mold on the skin of the planet. I've got hummingbird feeders to fill, a shelf of cookbooks to plow through, and diverting fiction to read. Friends keep me posted on essential movies I must view and there is always the music thundering off the radio. When I leave Juárez and go to various cities in the United States, it simply ceases to exist, even if I only travel thirty feet across the river into El Paso. I used to wonder about this fact.

I'm sitting in Jaime Murrieta's beat-up old car and he is rifling through a box of his photographs. Murrieta is a man of boundless energy, his face does not so much smile as gleam, and he is electric with pleasure as he plows through some of his favorite things. He flings things at me in no particular order. He is a lover of Juárez in all its faces and disguises. Like most Mexicans, he is extremely patriotic. Beneath the contempt for government and the police and the corruption, there always looms this love of country. Jaime is square-built and always seems to be on the balls of his feet, an athlete ready to spring. This day he has taken a few blows shooting a gathering of narcotraficantes, but this pummeling has not dented his good spirits. I hold the negatives of this shoot up to the light. Then he tosses me some prints of a prizefight, a series of shots of ring girls looking ungainly as they strut in their high heels holding up cards with the round number.

He hands me a shot of his face after a beating. His features are puffy, his face semicomatose. I look over at Jaime and he is beaming as if the photograph brought back all the pleasure of that moment. See, his eyes seem to say, they did this to me but they did not stop me.

Sometimes I drift into a fantasy about a whore I met in Juárez and the life we will build together. Her name is Adriana and one night over drinks in a club she told me how she had worked in the maquilas but discovered the pay was not sufficient. Now she works on her back and her two kids eat. The face is fresh, the eyes flint, the hips curved, and the stomach sagging under the work. She is a good-looking woman who never got to be a girl and now thinks she will never get to be a person. In my fantasy, Adriana and I do the right thing and follow the instructions of our time. We build a small casa by the sea. Actually, she has wrapped up her graduate studies at the National Autonomous University of México, UNAM. She has an M.A. in romance languages and, of course, an M.B.A., plus a doctorate in anthropology awarded for her groundbreaking study, "Sex-

Ernesto Rodríguez. *Illegal immigrants arrested in El Paso by the U.S. Border Patrol. The arrest has taken place as part of Operation Hold the Line.*

ual Surrogates: Free Trade, Multi-Culturalism and the Feminist Perspective." She is now preparing a dictionary of the industrial argot in her work for a journal of linguistics and is contemplating a study of dialogues with clients utilizing the full French critical apparatus. We have given our future some thought, constructed a portfolio, laid down Keoghs and other goodies, and divided housework in a contractual manner. The children will play on the beach, I'll keep a watchful eye on them because the undertow here is terrific. Each morning she and I will jog up and down the sands and the pounds will melt off her and restore her girlish figure. We will live on locust, wild honey, young goat, fresh fruits, vitamin supplements, garlic tablets, and various hot salsas. She will quit her trade and devote her time to shopping and come home each day with the minivan crammed with bags and packages. Of course she will ferry the kids to their soccer matches. The satellite dish will keep us informed and in a fine torpor. We will watch waves and make love in the water. Our children will be taught at home and they will learn seven languages, two of them dead and classical since you never know what will turn up. Groceries will be home-delivered and the only "Made in the U.S.A." will be me. I will become gentle and kindly and after

a time I will question nothing. My work will be constant meetings at a nearby academy and I will fight like a junkyard dog for tenure. Of course we will pay our taxes and vote. We intend to make this arrangement work. In the evening we will consider the virtues of various health plans and lecture our young on safe sex and no sex and why have sex at all. They will be raised without tasting salt or unseemly fats. We are adamant on this last point. She will secretly slip them candy but there is nothing I can do about this fact.

Why should I take the risk of messing up my life?

We will call it love but don't worry, we will seek counseling.

I go back to the glowing screen in the dark room one more time. I must see that blackened face again. Soft music calms me, the blackness of the room caresses me, the roar of the fan on the projector is oddly comforting. The beam of the white light defines reality now and keeps it locked up within a rectangle. Jaime Bailleres installs a slide carousel and then I hear a click and color explodes. The photographers do not know if this is art. It is not for them to say. Nada qué ver. I face again the open mouth and clean white teeth.

"Why do you want this picture?" Jaime Bailleres asks me. "You know it will never be published. No one will print it."

I have never told him the truth. I have never told him that the first night I saw the girl's face I thought it was a carved wooden mask, something made by one of those quaint tribes far away in the Mexican south. Nor have I told him that I keep a Xerox copy of it in a folder right by where I work and from time to time I open that clean manila folder and look into her face. And then I close it like the lid of a coffin.

Ernesto Rodríguez. *One of the many young workers in the maquiladora industry who was kidnapped, raped, and murdered. Young women generally between the ages of sixteen and twenty-four disappear, their mutilated bodies being discovered later in the Lote Bravo, buried in the desert sand.*

She haunts me and I deal with this fact by avoiding it. I have brought a pile of photography books to Jaime's house to add to the communal archive maintained by the street shooters of Juárez. We are all here at this moment, sitting in the room staring at the screen. Manny Sáenz has just finished showing me huge prints of his work. Alfredo Carrillo is autographing those black-and-white photographs he wishes to give me. Julián Cardona has brought a bottle of wine for me—one twelve years old. I am haggling with Gabriel Cardona over a print. We are amigos now. I have rustled up a curio—a bottle of wine called NAFTA with the label Mexican, the wine U.S., and the bottle Canadian. Everyone smiles at this farcical vintage. The photographers tell me after we have been drinking for hours, "You give us hope." It must be the wine.

I look up at Jaime Bailleres, the girl's face is still floating on the screen, his question about my interest in the photograph hangs in the air.

"Yes," I tell him, "You are right. No one will ever print this photograph. But I want them to see it whether they print it or not."

He sighs, the way an adult sighs over the actions of a child.

I look up at the girl on the screen. I tell myself a photograph is worth a thousand words. I tell myself photographs lie. I tell myself there are lies, damned lies, and statistics. I tell myself I am still sleeping. But she stares at me. The skin is smooth, almost carved and sanded, but much too dark. And the screams are simply too deafening.

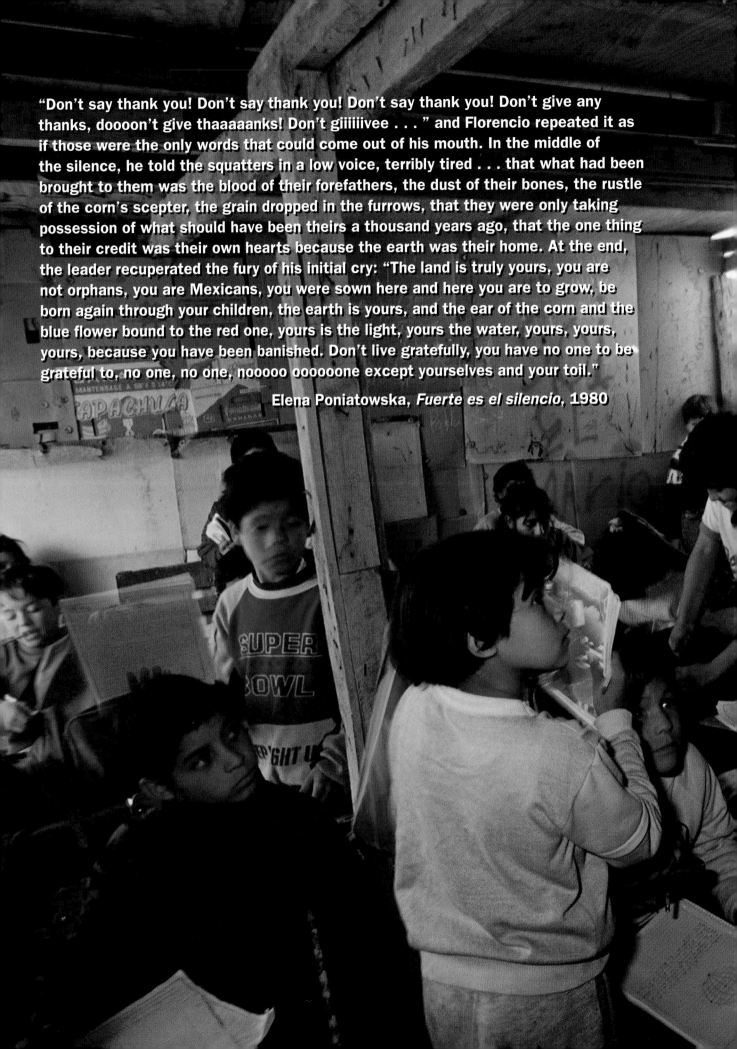

"Don't say thank you! Don't say thank you! Don't say thank you! Don't give any thanks, doooon't give thaaaaanks! Don't giiiiiivee . . . " and Florencio repeated it as if those were the only words that could come out of his mouth. In the middle of the silence, he told the squatters in a low voice, terribly tired . . . that what had been brought to them was the blood of their forefathers, the dust of their bones, the rustle of the corn's scepter, the grain dropped in the furrows, that they were only taking possession of what should have been theirs a thousand years ago, that the one thing to their credit was their own hearts because the earth was their home. At the end, the leader recuperated the fury of his initial cry: "The land is truly yours, you are not orphans, you are Mexicans, you were sown here and here you are to grow, be born again through your children, the earth is yours, and the ear of the corn and the blue flower bound to the red one, yours is the light, yours the water, yours, yours, yours, because you have been banished. Don't live gratefully, you have no one to be grateful to, no one, no one, nooooo oooooone except yourselves and your toil."

Elena Poniatowska, *Fuerte es el silencio*, 1980

4. THERE IS DOUBLE EXPOSURE

There is a line we say we will not cross and yet that line must always be crossed if we are to live a life and have a death. This commonplace is seldom noted and almost always lied about. We erect barriers and we call these barriers disciplines

or professions or, sometimes in the name of God Almighty, ethics. And these barriers keep us on one side of the line and keep what we see and feel and sense and fear on the other side of the line. In my work—writing, reporting, whatever—they call it objectivity, and you are judged and rewarded according to how closely you cling to this thing called objectivity. For the photographers it is much the same, they are paid to hold cameras in their hands, snap images, and be blank pathways between what they see and what the film captures. That is the theory. The practice is faces, smiles, screams, sounds, smells, and these things, these forces radiating off the subjects will not stay on one side of the camera and will not keep to their places on one side of the line and they cross and then what are we to do? And if they cross that line, what will they do to us? How can we keep our distance when what we are seeing and talking about is closing the distance between us? How can we ever avoid double exposure?

In Juárez, things happen and yet do not. The crack of a pistol breaks the glass of social peace, the thirsty slicing of a knife frees a river of blood, the thud of

fists on flesh tattoos a rhythm on the city. And then come horror, photographs, momentary outcries, and inevitably a blanket of silence that smothers all events. It is the same for the photographers. So we will look at matters outside the frame of the 35mm camera, the film known but never developed or printed.

There is a killing ground that North American eyes are culturally trained not to see and on this ground things change but seem never to get better. The history of the United States for the most part, and the national fable in every version, is this: things get better. In México and many other parts of the world this belief is absent. After World War II, the Mexican miracle occurred, which means that for twenty years or so wages rose but as often as not did not keep up with inflation. After the miracle, things got worse. Around 1958, the richest 5 percent of the nation earned twenty-two times the income of the poorest 10 percent. At the beginning of the '80s, the economic leaders in the top 5 percent were bagging fifty times the share given the bottom 10 percent. Then with economic collapse in 1982, the real hard times began. Wages sank, and by 1987 inflation chugged along at 150 percent. With the fraudulent election of Carlos Salinas de Gortari in 1988, several things happened over the next six years: inflation was crushed, real wages fell by about a third, NAFTA was passed, and México entered the world of free trade. Then in December

Pages 106–107: Gabriel Cardona. *School in Colonia Primero de Mayo.*
Opposite: Ernesto Rodríguez. *A Mexican former police officer, who had allegedly been involved in car theft, was executed on a main street in Cd. Juárez by narcotraficantes. It was broad daylight and he was making a phone call, his wife at his side.*

1994, the peso and the economy collapsed still further. Since then there have been many announcements from Mexican and U.S. authorities that all the economic indicators are looking good. What Mexicans see and taste is captured in the photographs you see in this book.

In the last fifteen years, forty Mexican journalists have been murdered, according to officials. The Ibero-American University, a Jesuit school in México City, calculates that every forty-eight hours a Mexican reporter is attacked or harassed, and every ninety days one is slaughtered. Since President Ernesto Zedillo assumed office in December 1994 promising reform and an opening toward democracy, eleven reporters have been murdered, 125 attacked, nine kidnapped. And seventy-four tortured. Of course, many incidents, perhaps most, are never reported. México is the champion in all of Latin America for murdered reporters and in the top fourteen worldwide. The real number is anyone's guess. In late 1996, two reporters and their three children were clubbed to death in their home in México City after publishing material about a major drug cartel. Law and order being what it is, the couple's servants were arrested for the murder and the press was informed that the dead husband and father had raped the maid. This may be true or this may be a lie: we are unlikely ever to know conclusively. Next story.

It is early January 1997 and a Juárez photographer goes into a fine district of the city to shoot fancy houses for his newspaper. He disappears. Amado Carrillo Fuentes, then boss of the Juárez cartel, owns five or six homes in that area. Two days later the missing photographer's family—an ailing mother and half a dozen poverty-stricken siblings—go to the police. Several days after that, more than one hundred Juárez journalists petition the governor to look into the matter. The journalists tell the governor that the "climate of violence" in the city is part of the problem. They place a one-page ad in the local newspaper protesting the disappearance and the sea of violence that laps across the city. One evening the missing photographer magically reappears. He tells the authorities he was kidnapped, tortured, and beaten. This story fails to win over his audience. So he then tells the authorities that what he really did was sell his camera and gear and go to the Pacific Coast, where he sprawled on the beach for a week or so. The authorities like this second story. Shortly thereafter this photographer leaves Juárez for sanctuary in a place far to the south. The newspaper duns the local reporters and photographers for the price of the ad they had plunked into the daily paper. And then comes the silence.

México has a tendency to disappear, just like that photographer, just like the dead girls, just like the hundreds of foreign-owned factories paying miserable wages. It can disappear because we do not want to face it. And we do not want to face it because it is a big problem for which we have no answers that we are eager to live with. México is the bridge to the twenty-first century and we are terrified of crossing this bridge. We prefer to retreat into the theology of global capitalism, a gibberish that is unintelligible yet soothing since it says: things will work out somehow. Once in a while, we crack and sputter a few words.

This breakdown can happen to any of us, even the best and the brightest: "I came to this job committed to restoring the middle-class and I did everything I knew to do. We lowered the deficit. We increased investment in education, in technology, in research and development. We expanded trade frontiers. We have seven million more jobs. We have a record number of millionaires. We have an all-time high stock market. We have more new businesses than ever before. . . . And most people are still working harder for lower pay than they were making the day I was sworn in as President. . . . How did this happen? We're moving into a global economy, an information society. . . . These income trends are huge, huge trends, huge, sweeping over two decades, fast international forces behind them, trillions of dollars of money moving across international borders working to find the lowest labor cost and pressing down, untold improvements in automation. . . . So fast that you can't create enough high-wage jobs to overcome the ones that are being depressed in some sectors of the economy." The man talking out his troubles is named William Jefferson Clinton.

That's the way it looks in the lab. Until we look away once again.

It is Thursday night and I am sitting in a nice bar with a Mexican photographer. I am very happy because he is happy, and for reasons I cannot fathom but truly envy, he is a man who is always happy. This very morning he went to the city hall of Juárez on assignment and when he came out he found this note stuck under the windshield wiper of his car: "You are going to get bullets for your photos. Watch out asshole." The photographer laughs as he tells me of the message. Many consider him kind of crazy because he does not seem to care whether he lives or dies. He has collected for me many photographs of his work over the last six or twelve months. I have flipped through his prints. Fire has come to Juárez. In the spring of 1996, a man burned the head off another man by placing it in a tipped barrel and starting a fire. Then two or three months ago, necklacing—the placement of a tire around the neck, and then the match—showed up. A woman surfaces—the body burned and then the bones burned also. A friend of mine believes these bones come from a woman he knows. Or knew.

We drink and I try not to think about the images. In part, I've had a bellyful of gore. In part, I can hear the voices saying this is not typical of our community, these things happen everywhere, some sections of some American cities are worse. Within twenty-four hours a public forum will be held at which I will be soundly denounced for writing of such matters. Within twenty-four hours the mayor of Juárez will go on television to point out that I am a liar smearing a fine city. The photographer has spent the day with a New York television producer who wishes to do a documentary on the factory workers, the poverty, the violence, the look of things in this place. We order another round—sometimes alcohol seems to be the only glue that can hold this city together.

Julián Cardona. *Soledad Batista, the Tarahumara candidate for the ecological party, Partido Verde Ecologista de México (PVEM), pickets in front of the state government representation office and discusses Governor Francisco Barrio's repression of the Tepehuanes and Tarahumara Indians.*

I am resigned to nothing but accepting of much. I know in order to protect him I cannot write the real name and dates of the photographer who vanished and then reappeared. And I know of other incidents I cannot write here at all. I know I should not write the name of the smiling man with the death-threat note sitting beside me in this saloon. I accept this condition. I have a videotape taken in the local prison of the man who put another man's head in a barrel and then burned it off. In the tape he speaks calmly of his life and his crime. In the same tape, some drug guys in the jail show off their cell with its kitchen, television, VCR, and other refinements. The jail's transvestites are putting on a musical show. I accept the condition. But I am not resigned. I do not know how to shrug.

I am looking right now at a wavy print taken from one of La Pantera's videotapes. A man with a full face, a receding hairline, a small nose, and full cheeks is lying down in this print. His mouth is stuffed with paper, a sign that he should not have talked. The man is dead. This condition I do not accept. It is time for everyone to talk. It is time for everyone to talk despite the thickets of racism, of foreign-policy considerations, of the growing and ominous military presence on the border, of the barbarism festering in our agencies that expresses itself in the mistreatment of illegal immigrants from México. It is time to talk because silence only makes matters worse, bodies cold, murder sanctioned, and poverty invisible.

Another photograph. She is serene, the lips full, the chin strong, a thick head of hair lying on the brown desert dirt. She wears a white blouse tied in a knot just under her rib cage, white striped trousers, and a face that says peace. Two men stand by her, one in brown trousers, the other in blue, both cut off at the knees. The sun dapples her face. Blood streams from her nostril, still red and vibrant in its freshness. She is an American who now lies dead on Mexican soil outside Juárez. She looks asleep, the lipstick red and perfectly applied. I peer at the photograph under a magnifying glass. I expect her to rise up, yawn, and speak. She will not, of course, but still I expect it. She is one of the many dead, individuals executed and dumped in the desert because of bad luck or carelessness or unforgivable error. But she looks very human, not unlike you or I, and for that reason she is not so easy to dismiss. She is one of us and we must face this fact and face this serene face.

I caution a magazine in New York about the dead woman with the serene face and suggest that given the circumstances they put a black bar over her features. They do not and the photograph goes into the press. A week or so later the editor receives a call from an American city where the brother of the dead girl lives. He talks long and hard and he tells the editor that by printing that photograph he is going to get the caller killed and his brothers and sisters killed and their children killed and his parents killed. The editor calls me up. Now the photographs are suddenly real.

It is time to talk and the photographs are the talking points. They are singular and actual. They are metaphors for nothing. They slap us in the face. They are Juárez and now Juárez exists in many places, and until we have the courage and decency to speak, Juárez will plant itself in yet more places. Juárez is the future, but the future, in part, is in our hands and we can make of it what we will. But first we must look and speak.

This is not easy under the night sky of Juárez with the sounds of the city clanging in the air. The photographers are standing around me and we talk and laugh and never relax. A car pulls down the street and we all glance in an automatic response and yet say nothing about this gesture. Two men walk past and we watch them warily. It is the alertness of any city, perhaps, yet more keenly felt here. Sometimes we acknowledge this fact, sometimes we do not. I remember one night after hours of talk and drinks and tales, one photographer erupted with fury and said that a block from his house they sell drugs under the street lamps and guns fire and . . . and what? That is the problem. What exactly should the next sentence be? Things are . . . to be known, to be ignored, to be denied, but still, things are. So we stand in the street as the night swirls around us and we ignore the night, and yet always feel its hand on our shoulders.

This is what it feels like when that cold hand touches our shoulders: imagine it is night and you have a poor job and little money and you are walking down a lonely city street with garbage strewn about the sidewalk and suddenly out of nowhere a

Jaime Murrieta. *Narco execution.*

huge fleet of limousines races past, the long stretch bodies gleaming, the windows tinted dark, and the occupants obscure. The tires slash through puddles and splash you. And then they are gone and you forget it ever happened. You feel your wet clothing and think there must have been a light shower that you did not notice. That is the walk we all now make each evening.

Or we do not. I am talking with someone at *The New York Times* and I am told, No, no, it is not that way, things are looking up, any economic change entails some dislocations, things will work out, and it is not as bad as some say, certainly not the way I say. I am told to look at the numbers. And I understand the feeling, I know how good a full belly feels and the crackle of the stiff paper of a freshly minted

check, a rectangle screaming money that comes like clockwork every two weeks. And I understand how easy it is, even once you know or at least sense the knowing, to turn away and forget or move on and not recognize what you have glimpsed or tasted. So we continue talking for the better part of an hour and agree to disagree, and I hang up with the feeling that things look somewhat differently in Times Square, as they always have. I remember saying, just before the end of the conversation, we will see. I believe we will.

But what we see depends on whether we open our eyes. In the early morning hours of 4 July 1997, Amado Carrillo Fuentes reclines in the bed of a maternity ward in México City and dies. The previous day he spent eight or nine hours having blubber sucked out of his gut and the lines and folds and wrinkles of his face restructured into a new look. Two body-

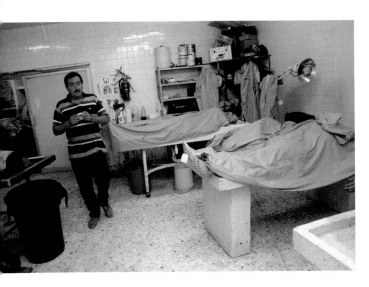

Above: Julián Cardona. *At 9:30 P.M. on 3 August 1997, four men driving a black Jaguar with Texas plates arrived at the restaurant Max fim, on Cd. Juárez's main street, Paseo Triunfo de la Republica, and with AK-47s executed six people. Those murdered included Alfonso Corral Oláguez, allegedly a narcotraficante.*
Opposite: Jaime Bailleres. *Three men were shot to death and two wounded outside of Geronimo's Bar and Grill on 31 August 1997.*

guards stood watch in the surgery room while the doctors toiled, and then he was wheeled to a hospital floor where he had purchased each and every room. The Mexican press reports he died of a heart attack or he died from being smothered with a pillow or he died from being strangled or he died from being administered the wrong drug. Or he did not die. There is talk of a body swap. There is talk that he has become a DEA informant and is being hidden. There is talk that he has a new life on a beach somewhere and drinks cool, refreshing potions. And there is talk that he was the kingpin of the drug world and his death means a victory and now things will get better for the good guys. But no one talks about the fact that whether Amado Carrillo Fuentes is alive or dead the business goes on and all that the business entails goes on. A few days after Carrillo dies or does not die, the American government announces a new report on NAFTA and finds small gains and beckoning horizons. This conclusion is also saluted by the nation's policymakers and it also begs the ques-

tions posed by the Juárezes of the world. The maquilas are still there, the pollution, the hopeless wages, the poverty, the grind of life. The report cannot change this reality and so ignores it. That is how we stay sane—by saying Carrillo is dead or Carrillo is not that important, by saying NAFTA is a boon or NAFTA is whatever but is not that important. We glide over things rather than look at things.

This will work for a while, until the things start looking back at us.

What we now think is not true. What we now do no longer works. What we see in the photographs actually exists. This is not darkness at the edge of town. This is going to be our town. And not because the dreaded Mexicans are coming but because we are planting ruin about the world and calling it our economic policy. We must stop pretending and start living. We already have lives of double exposure. Just as the photographers cannot really stay on one side of the camera, we cannot really stay on one side of the line. We will cross it, we have crossed it, we are in play. We have many options and none of them are easy. But the one option we do not have is to continue our past habits into the future. We cannot pretend such places do not exist. We cannot pretend such places can be contained. We cannot pretend such places will magically remedy themselves. We are exposed and we should be. And we are exposed to the future and this future will be hard, but it can also be good or bad depending upon what we do. We are free to act. If we act in time.

It is a very old story. We must treat people as we wish to be treated. Forget the theology of free trade, forget the theology of foreign policy, forget the theology of immigration reform, forget the theology of the military. They will not answer to the task. Look into the faces, stare at the huts, wince at the murders, think of the numbers. Then the choices will be simple. And the price of a bad choice will be obvious.

If people are paid less than they can live on, they will eventually either die or act to stay alive. If they

are stashed in factories for six days a week, they will eventually organize. If the people who work in the factories are drawn to the border, they will eventually cross. Or erupt and spread like lava. The rest is details of labor laws or lack of laws, of international agreements or lack of agreements, of well-intentioned employers or ill-intentioned employers. Such details can influence the rate of the action but cannot really alter the action. Just as vice and murder and despair cannot really alter the action. If people are gathered together and then punished for gathering by fences, or paid slave wages, or robbed by crooked governments, then they eventually act. It does not matter if these acts, when they come, are kindly or savage, sensible or insane, they will come. Nor does it matter if the men and women and children who have been drawn to the border wish change or desire violence, or dread change and dread violence.

The change will come as the colonias appear one by one, as the shacks spread up the hillside one by one, as the wall extends itself along the line one mile by one mile. No one knows when, just as none of us know if we will be in the face of the storm. We just know in our hearts and in our guts that it will come. This time we will not even know what to call it, because in the twentieth century we've used up all the names: progress, revolt, revolution, terrorism, wars of national liberation, genocide. We have exhausted our language trying to paper over with words what we know will come. We are left with tattered words and we use these words to describe or dismiss the bad places where machetes cut off heads, where trenches serve as mass graves, where plague leaps from the forest and runs wild and free, singing through the cells of our bodies. But the words ring hollow. No one hopes for revolution just as no one really thinks that capitalism can, all by itself, right social wrongs or fairly distribute the treasure created by labor. Progress is a word now left for the comedians. Our last refuge is cyberspace and we all know cyberspace is an imaginary entity, the region we call virtual reality, where no one has a name and the women and children do what we desire and rumor serves as fact. Something else is knocking at our door. Something riding a search engine beyond the dreams or nightmares of our software wizards. We can hear it coming. And we can see it in the photographs. Listen, look. It comes now, nameless for the time being, formless at the moment, but expected. Briefly, so briefly, frozen in the frame and printed on the page.

I look at the café in the desert sunset. The lights have just come on and the lonely roadhouse in the dunes thirty or forty miles out of Juárez glows as the night comes down. Semis blur past and the café looks like the clean, well-lit room we all think we seek for succor. All this exists in a print that one of the photographers has given me because, he explains, I love deserts. And he is right. The hot, dry winds, the cold nights, dead streams, and blue skies anchor me. I stand in Juárez under a street light and look at the print as the photographer smiles at me and I thank him for a touchstone as two million people claw their way toward survival and tomorrow in the acres around me.

We already know enough to ask the right questions. And the right questions are always the beginning of the answers.

Welcome to the laboratory of our future.

Opposite top: Gabriel Cardona. *On 23 August 1997, four doctors were found strangled to death. They had left the hospitals where they worked to attend an unknown patient who had been wounded by gunfire. It is believed that this patient was a narcotraficante, and that those who lured the doctors to his aid killed them to erase evidence. In the month following the supposed death of Amado Carrillo Fuentes, "El Señor de los Cielos" (The lord of the skies), there were at least twelve narco-related murders in Cd. Juárez.*
Opposite bottom: Gabriel Cardona. *This man's mummified skin suggests that he had been dead for at least a month before being found, on 9 August 1997. Police in the area are constantly finding bodies, often those of victims of gang- or drug-related executions.*
Pages 118–119: Manuel Sáenz. *In this image, "Spider Man," a young Mexican climbs over the metal border fence at the Puente Negro to cross into El Paso for work.*

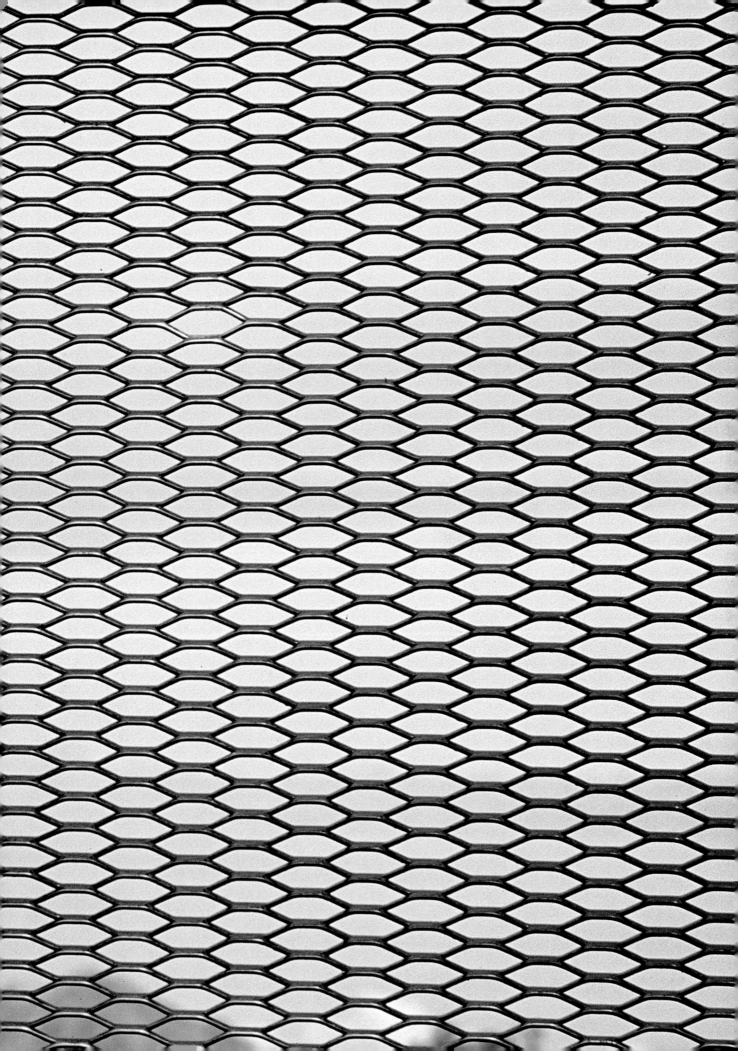

To Be Like Them

BY EDUARDO GALEANO

Dreams and nightmares are made of the same material. But this nightmare purports to be the only dream we're allowed: a development model that scorns life and idolizes things.

Can We Be Like Them?

Promise of politicians, rationale of technocrats, fantasy of the forsaken: the Third World will become like the First World, rich, cultured, and happy, if only it behaves itself and does what it's told without kidding around or asking embarrassing questions. In the final episode of the soap opera called History, prosperity will reward the good behavior of those dying of hunger. *We can be like them*, announces the gigantic neon sign that lights the pathway to the development of the underdeveloped and the modernization of the backward.

But *what can't be, can't be, and besides it's impossible*, as Pedro the Cock, a bullfighter, put it. If poor countries rise to the level of production and waste of the wealthy, the planet will die. Our unlucky planet is already in a coma, poisoned by industrial civilization and squeezed to the next-to-the-last drop by consumer society.

In the last twenty years, while humanity tripled in number, erosion killed off the equivalent of all the arable land in the United States. The world, transformed into market and merchandise, is losing fifteen million hectares of forest each year. Of these, six million become desert. Nature has been humili-

Jaime Bailleres. *Many of the poorest barrios in Cd. Juárez are shrouded in pollution. Their residents generally work at one of the maquiladoras, making at most the equivalent of around $50 a week (detail of original photograph).*

ated and subordinated to the accumulation of capital. Land, water, and air are being poisoned so that money will generate more money without a drop in the rate of profit. Efficient is he who earns more in less time.

In the North, acid rain from industrial smoke is killing off woods and lakes, while toxic wastes poison rivers and seas. And in the South, export agribusiness marches on, obliterating trees and people. North and south, east and west, people are sawing away with delirious enthusiasm at the very branch on which they sit.

From forest to desert: modernization, devastation. The incessant bonfire of the Amazon consumes half a Belgium a year. In all of Latin America, land is peeling away and drying up—twenty-two hectares of forest die *every minute*, most of it sacrificed by the companies that produce meat or wood on a grand scale to be consumed elsewhere. Costa Rican cows turn into McDonald's hamburgers. Half a century ago, trees covered three-quarters of that small country; few are left today. At the current rate of deforestation, Costa Rica will be bald by the end of the century. Costa Rica exports meat to the United States, and imports from the same place pesticides that the United States bans from its own soil.

A few countries squander resources that belong to everyone. Crime and delirium of the society of waste: the richest 6 percent of humanity devours a third of all the energy and a third of all the natural resources consumed in the world. Statistical averages show that one North American consumes as much as fifty Haitians. Of course, such averages can't summon up a resident of Harlem or Baby Doc Duvalier, but it's still worth asking: What would happen if the fifty Haitians suddenly consumed as much as fifty North Americans? What would happen if the immense population of the South devoured the world with the voracious impunity of the North? What would happen if luxury goods and automobiles and refrigerators and TV sets and nuclear power plants and electrical generating stations proliferated in the South in such a crazy fashion? In ten years all the oil in the world would be used up. And what would happen to the climate, which is already close to collapse from global warming? What would happen to the land, the little bit left after erosion? And the water, which a fourth of humanity is already drinking contaminated by nitrates and pesticides and industrial waste laced with mercury and lead? What would happen? It wouldn't happen. We would have to move to another planet. This one, worn so thin already, couldn't handle it.

The precarious equilibrium of the world, which teeters on the brink of the abyss, depends on the perpetuation of injustice. The misery of many makes possible the extravagance of the few. For a few to continue consuming more, many must continue consuming less. And to make sure the many don't cross the line, the system multiplies the weapons of war. Incapable of fighting poverty, the system fights the poor, and its culture—dominant and militarized—blesses the violence of power.

The American way of life, founded on the right to waste, can only be lived by dominant minorities in dominated countries. Its adoption en masse would be the collective suicide of humanity.

It's not possible. But would it be desirable?

Do We Want To Be Like Them?
In a well-organized anthill, the queens are few and the workers many. Queens are born with wings and can make love. Workers, who neither fly nor love, work for the queens. The police ants keep watch over the workers and the queens.

Life is what happens to you while you're busy making other plans, said John Lennon. In our age, marked as it is by the confusion of means and ends, people don't work to live: they live to work. Some work more and more because they need more than they consume; and others work more and more to continue consuming more than they need.

It seems quite normal that in Latin America the eight-hour day belongs to the dominions of abstract art. Second jobs, which official statistics rarely admit, are the reality for very many who would otherwise go hungry. But is it normal that people at the peak of development should work like ants? Does wealth bring freedom, or does it intensify the fear of freedom?

To be is to have, says the system. And the system is a trap: the more you have, the more you want; people end up belonging to things and working for them. Consumer lifestyle, which is becoming the only lifestyle anywhere, makes time a scarce and expensive resource: time is sold, rented, invested. But who is the owner of time? Automobiles, television sets, VCRs, personal computers, cellular phones, and all the other countersigns of happiness. Machines, created *to save time* or *to pass the time*, seize control of time. Take the case of the automobile: not only does it rule urban space, it rules human time. In theory, cars *economize time*, but in practice they devour it. A good portion of work time goes to paying for transportation to and from the job, which in itself takes up more and more time because of the traffic jams in our modern Babylons.

You do not have to be an economic genius. Common sense tells us that technological progress, by increasing productivity, diminishes the time that must be devoted to work. But common sense didn't foresee the fear of *free time*, or the traps of consumerism, or the manipulative power of advertising. In Japan, people have worked forty-seven hours a week for the past twenty years. Europe's workdays have shrunk, but very slowly, at a pace that has nothing to do with the accelerated development of productivity. In automated factories, there are ten workers where once there were a thousand, but instead of broadening the arena of freedom, technological progress generates unemployment. The freedom *to waste time*: consumer society doesn't allow for such waste. Even vacations, organized by the large companies that industrialized tourism, have become an exhausting pursuit. *To kill time*: modern vacation spots reproduce the vertigo of daily life in the urban anthill.

According to the anthropologists, our Paleolithic ancestors worked no more than twenty hours a week. According to the newspapers, our contemporaries in Switzerland voted at the end of 1988 on a measure to reduce the work week to forty hours without cutting salaries. And the Swiss voted it down.

Ants communicate by touching antennae. TV antennae communicate with centers of power in the modern world. The little screen offers us the urge to own, the frenzy to consume, the excitement of competition, and the anxious yearning to succeed, just as Columbus offered baubles to the Indians. Successful merchandise. Advertising fails to tell us, however, that according to the World Health Organization, the United States consumes *nearly half of all the tranquilizers sold on the planet*. In the last twenty years, the work week in the United States *increased*. During that period the number of people suffering from stress *doubled*.

The City as Gas Chamber

A peasant is worth less than a cow and more than a hen, I'm told in Caaguazú, Paraguay. And in the northeast of Brazil: *He who plants has not land, he who has land does not plant.*

Our fields empty out, Latin America's cities become hells as large as countries. México City grows at the rate of half a million people and thirty square kilometers *per year*; it already has five times as many inhabitants as all of Norway. By the end of the century, the capital of México and the Brazilian city of São Paulo will be the largest cities in the world.

The great cities of the South are like the great cities of the North viewed through a warped mirror. Modernization by mimicry increases the model's defects. Latin America's raucous smoke-filled capital cities have no bicycle lanes or catalytic converters to filter out toxic fumes. Clean air and silence are so rare and expensive that not even the richest of the rich can buy them.

The Brazilian subsidiaries of Volkswagen and Ford make cars without catalytic converters for sale in Brazil and other Latin American countries. They make them with converters in Germany and the United States. Argentina produces unleaded gasoline for export and poisonous gasoline for the internal market. In all of Latin America, automobiles have the freedom to vomit lead from their exhaust pipes. From the cars' point of view, lead raises the octane level and the rate of profit. From people's point of view, lead damages the brain and the nervous system. Cars, the true owners of cities, pay no attention to the intruders.

The year 2000, memories of the future: people with oxygen masks, birds that cough instead of sing, trees that refuse to grow. Right now in México City you see signs that say: *We beg of you not to bother the walls* and *Please don't slam the door*. There are still no signs that say: *Breathing not advisable*. How long will it be before such public health warnings appear? Cars and factories offer up to the atmosphere 11,000 tons of enemy gases and fumes every day. There is a cloud of filth in the air, children are born with lead in their blood, and on more than one occasion, dead birds have rained down over this city, which, until half a century ago, was *the most transparent region on earth*. Now this cocktail of carbon monoxide, sulfur dioxide, and nitrogen oxide can be as high as three times the maximum tolerable to human beings. What will be the maximum tolerable to urban beings?

Five million cars: the city of São Paulo has been defined as a sick person on the verge of a heart attack. A cloud of fumes masks it. Only on Sunday can you see, from the outskirts, the most developed city of

Brazil. On downtown avenues, electric billboards warn the population every day:

Air quality: ruin

According to the testing stations, in 1986 the air was dirty or very dirty on 323 days.

In June 1989, for a few rainless and windless days, Santiago de Chile vied with México City and São Paulo for the world pollution championship. San Cristóbal Hill in downtown Santiago was invisible, hidden behind a mask of smog. Chile's young democratic government took a few minimal steps to control the 800 tons of fumes that spew into the city's air each day. The cars and the factories screamed to the high heavens: those limitations violated business freedom and infringed on the right of property. Money's freedom, which scorns everyone else's, knew no bounds during the dictatorship of General Pinochet, and made a worthy contribution to poisoning everything. The right to pollute is a fundamental incentive to foreign investment, almost as important as the right to pay tiny salaries. And after all, General Pinochet never denied Chileans the right to breathe shit.

The City as Jail

Consumer society, which consumes people, obliges people to consume, while television offers courses on violence to the learned and the illiterate alike. Those who have nothing may live far away from those who have everything, but every day they spy on them through the little screen. Television exhibits the obscene extravagance of the orgy of consumption, and at the same time teaches the art of shooting your way in.

Pages 124–125: Manuel Sáenz. In the polluted Rio Grande, children fish for food for their families.
Above right: Manuel Sáenz. Yet another fire in El Paso's Chevron refinery, which is located in a residential area across the river from Cd. Juárez. People on both sides of the border are greatly alarmed by the idea that a fire here might become uncontainable.

Reality imitates TV, street violence is the continuation of television by other means. Street children practice private enterprise through crime, the only field open to them. Their only human rights are the right to rob and the right to die. Tiger cubs abandoned to their fate go on the hunt. On any corner they hit and run. Life comes to an early end, eaten up by glue and other drugs good for fooling hunger and cold and loneliness; or it ends when a bullet cuts it down.

To walk the streets of Latin America's large cities is risky, and so is staying home. *The city as jail*: he who is not a prisoner of need is a prisoner of fear. Those who have something, no matter how little, are condemned to live under threat, in terror of the next mugging. Those who have a lot live enclosed in secure fortresses. The great buildings and residential complexes are the feudal castles of the electronic era. It's true, they're missing the moats filled with crocodiles and the majestic beauty of the castles of the Middle Ages, but they've got the great raised bars, the high walls, the watchtowers, the armed guards.

The state, which is policelike rather than paternalistic, does not practice charity. Old-fashioned talk about reforming those who have gone astray by inculcating a belief in the virtues of study and work belongs to antiquity. In the epoch of market economies, the leftovers of the human breed are eliminated by hunger or the bullet. Street children, children of poor laborers, are not nor can they be *useful to society*. Education is the privilege of those who can pay for it; repression is the damnation of those who cannot.

According to *The New York Times*, between January and October 1990, the police murdered more than forty children in the streets of Guatemala City. The bodies of these children, beggar children, robber children, garbage-picking children, turned up without tongues, eyes, or ears, tossed in the dump. According to Amnesty International, during 1989, 457 children and adolescents were executed in the Brazilian cities of Rio de Janeiro, São Paulo, and Recife. These crimes, committed by death squads and other forces of the parapolice order, did not occur in backward rural areas, but in the most important cities of Brazil: they did not occur where capitalism is *lacking*, rather where *there is too much of it*. Social injustice and scorn for life grow along with the economy.

In countries where there is no death penalty, the death penalty is meted out every day in defense of the right of property. Opinion-makers tend to make apologies for crime. In the middle of 1990, in the city of Buenos Aires, an engineer shot two young thieves fleeing with the tape player from his car. Bernardo Neustadt, Argentina's most influential journalist, commented on television: *I would have done the same*. In the 1986 Brazilian elections, Afanásio Jazadji won a seat in the state congress of São Paulo in one of the greatest landslides in Brazil's history. Jazadji earned his immense popularity on the radio. His program loudly defended the death squads and preached in favor of torture and the extermination of delinquents.

In the civilization of savage capitalism, the right to own is more important than the right to live. People are worth less than things. In this sense, the laws of impunity are revealing. They absolved the state terrorism practiced by the military dictatorships of three countries in the South; they pardoned crime and torture; they did not pardon crimes against prop-

erty. (Chile: decree law 2191 of 1978. Uruguay: law 15.848 of 1986. Argentina: law 23.521 of 1987.)

The "Social Cost" of Progress

February 1989, Caracas. Bus fares suddenly soar to the skies, the price of bread triples, and an enraged people explodes: in the streets 300 lie dead, or 500, or who knows.

February 1991, Lima. A plague of cholera attacks the coasts of Peru, venting its fury on the port of Chimbote and the miserable slums of Lima and killing a hundred in a few days. The hospitals have no IV solution and no salt. The government's program of economic adjustment dismantled the little that was left of the public health system, and doubled in a flash the number of Peruvians living in extreme poverty. They earn less than the minimum wage, and the minimum wage is *$45 per month*.

Today's wars—electronic wars—take place on video game screens. The victims are neither seen nor heard. Neither does laboratory economics hear or see the scorched earth of the hungry. Remote-control weapons kill without remorse. The international technocracy, which imposes on the Third World its development programs and adjustment plans, also murders from outside and from afar.

For more that a quarter of a century, Latin America has been dismantling the fragile barriers that held off the arrogance of money. The creditor-bankers bombarded those defenses with the sure-shot weapon of extortion, while the governing military officers and politicians dynamited them from within. One after another they fall, the protective barriers raised by the state in other times. Now the state is selling off nationalized public enterprises for nothing, or worse than nothing because the seller pays. Our countries hand the keys and everything else over to the international monopolies, now called *price-formation factors*, and become free markets. In its wisdom, the international technocracy counsels injections for wooden legs and says the free market is the talisman of wealth. Why is it that rich countries, who preach the free market, do not practice it? This shrine of the weak is the most successful export of the strong. It's made for the consumption of poor countries. No rich country has ever used it.

Talisman of wealth for how many? Official statistics from Uruguay and Costa Rica, the two countries where social strife used to be least evident: now one of every six Uruguayans lives in extreme poverty, and two of every five Costa Rican families is poor.

The doubtful matrimony of supply and demand, in a free market that serves the despotism of the powerful, punishes the poor and generates a speculative economy. Production is discouraged, labor is scorned, consumption deified. The blackboards in foreign exchange houses are watched as if they were movie screens, the dollar is spoken of as if it were a person:

"And how is the dollar?"

Tragedy repeats itself as farce. Since the times of Christopher Columbus, Latin America has suffered capitalist development elsewhere as a tragedy of its own. Now it repeats as farce this caricature of development: a dwarf pretending to be a child.

The technocracy sees numbers and does not see people, but it only sees numbers that are convenient. At the end of this long quarter-century, some successes of *modernization* are celebrated. The *Bolivian miracle*, for example, fulfilled by virtue and courtesy of drug money: the cycle of tin has closed, and with the fall of tin came the end of the mining towns and the most combative labor unions of Bolivia. Now the people of Llallagua, who don't have drinking water, have a parabolic television antenna high up on Calvary Hill. Or the *Chilean miracle*, from the wonderful wizard of Chile, General Pinochet, a success sold as a potion in the countries of the East. But what was the price of the Chilean miracle? And who are the Chileans who paid it and continue to pay it? Who will be the Poles and Czechs and Hungarians who will pay it? In Chile, official statistics proclaim the proliferation of loaves, even while confessing to the proliferation of the hungry. The cock crows victory; the cackling is suspect. Could it be that failure has gone to its head? In 1970, 20 percent of all Chileans were poor. Today it's 45 percent.

The numbers confess, but they do not repent. After all, human dignity depends on the weighing of costs and benefits, and sacrificing the poor masses is nothing more that the *social cost* of Progress.

What might be the value of that *social cost*, if it could be measured? At the end of 1990, *Stern* magazine made a careful assessment of the damage caused by development in Germany today. The magazine estimated, in economic terms, the human and material cost of automobile accidents, traffic jams, air and water pollution, food contamination, the deterioration of green areas, and other factors, and concluded that the value of these damages was equivalent to a quarter of the entire gross national product. The spread of misery obviously was not included among the damages, because for the past several centuries Europe has fed its wealth on foreign poverty, but it would be interesting to know how far such an assessment would go if it were applied to the catastrophes of *modernization* in Latin America. In Germany the state controls and limits, up to a certain point, the noxious effects of the system on people and the environment. What would be the damage in countries like ours, which swallowed the story of the free market and let money move like a tiger on the loose? The damage done to us now and in the future by a system that fills our heads with artificial needs so that we forget our real needs—how accurately can it be assessed? Can the mutilation of the human soul be measured? The spread of violence, the debasement of daily life?

The West is living the euphoria of victory. The collapse of the East served up the vindication: in the East it was worse. Was it worse? Rather, I think, one should ask whether it was essentially *different*. In the West: justice sacrificed in the name of freedom, on the altar of the god of Productivity. In the East: freedom sacrificed in the name of justice, on the altar of the god of Productivity.

In the South, we still have the chance to ask ourselves if that god deserves our lives.

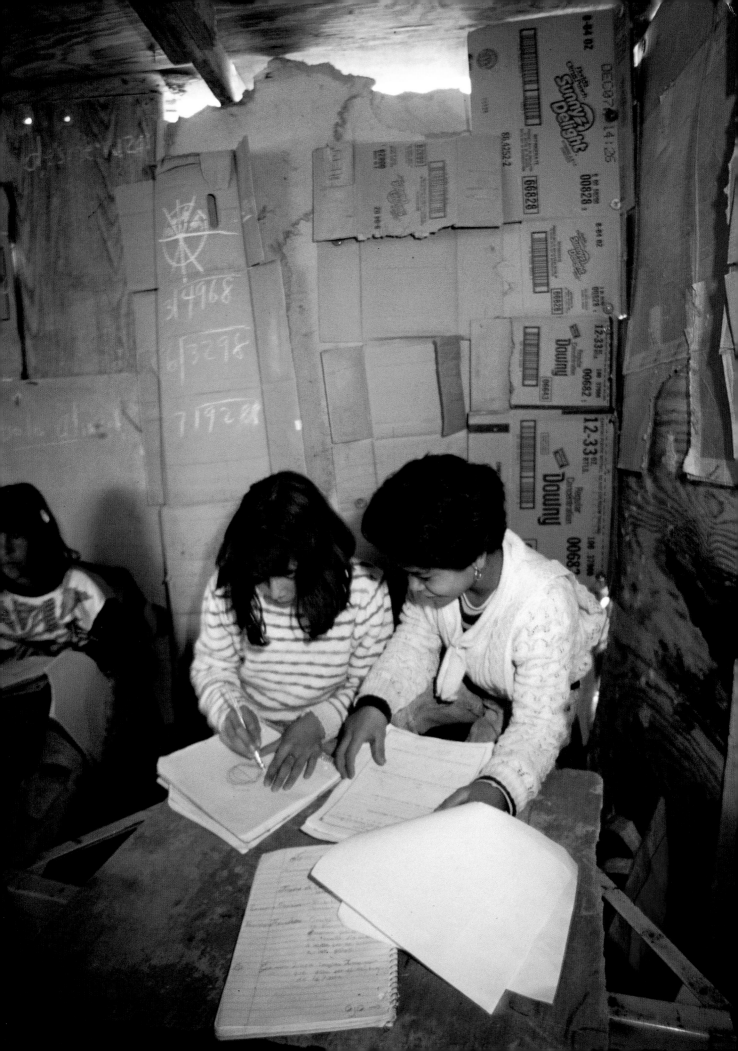

DEBTS

This book grew out of a story that originally appeared in *Harper's*, December 1996. I want to thank the folks there for printing it and my editor at *Harper's*, Clara Jeffery, for bearing with me. Some other parts of what I have written here have appeared in various disguises in *Terra Nova*, *GQ*, and God knows where else.

I want to thank Elena Poniatowska for her many thoughtful suggestions, my friend Carlos Vigueras for tolerating me, and Fellini for not killing me. The support of the Lannan Foundation has been singularly decent in a world where corporations and foundations generally share a common lack of nerve. The rest of what you hold in your hands is the work of Aperture and my editor there, Melissa Harris. She took a sad song and made it better. And hell, she is the only reason most of this song exists in print anyway. As publishing careens toward the commercially shallow and the academically toothless, Aperture is an extraordinary exception to this decline.

This book is about photographs and the photographs are about Juárez, and so I want to thank the photographers of Juárez for their work and for their dedication to the refreshing notion that capturing the world on film can help change the world.
—Charles Bowden

Opposite: Gabriel Cardona. *At the cardboard-and-wood Primero de Mayo school in Cd. Juárez, the fifth- and sixth-grade teacher is often lucky if she gets paid, let alone has proper materials to work with.*
Pages 132–133: Aurelio Suárez Núñez. *Colonia México 68, populated for the most part by members of the Partido del Trabajo, or PT (National party of workers).*
Page 135: Julián Cardona. *In an example of the underground economy in Cd. Juárez, two men dressed as clowns juggle at a busy intersection to earn money. Many prefer this kind of work—selling food or toys, doing small performances, washing windows—to working in a maquiladora for the equivalent of $4 or $5 a day.*

There is the story of how the great Russian poet Alexander Blok came to see his country estate during the Revolution that he himself had apocalyptically prophesied, and saw only ruins and ashes. Suddenly something flashed amidst the ruins. It was shattered pieces of a mirror that had fallen out of its burned walnut frame. He took the largest piece and walked about with it among the ashes the entire day, as though hoping that concealed in its depths was at least a tiny remainder of history. Red guards with a growth of stubble, as if they came straight from his poem "The Twelve," ordered the great poet to stop and hold the mirror for them while they shaved. The apostles of the Revolution, machine-gun belts crisscrossed on their chests, were displeased that the soot-blackened mirror obscured their faces full of revolutionary intransigence. Cursing, they wiped the mirror with their tattooed arms and the hems of their striped jerseys. And the poet continued on in his role of "saver of the mirror."

Yevgeny Yevtushenko,
"Foreword," *The Russian Century*, 1994

Unless otherwise noted, all excerpts from the following sources are copyright by and reprinted with permission from the author and/or publisher:

Endpaper: Oscar Lewis, *The Children of Sanchez*, copyright © 1961 by Oscar Lewis. Reprinted by permission of Harold Ober Associates Incorporated; p. 6: Elena Poniatowska, *Massacre in Mexico* (Columbia, MO: Univ. of Missouri Press, 1991, trans. Helen R. Lane); p. 8: Bob Dylan, "Just Like Tom Thumb's Blues," copyright © 1965 by Warner Bros. Music, copyright renewed © 1993 by Special Rider Music. All rights reserved. International copyright secured; p. 10: Elena Poniatowska, *Hasta no verte Jesús mío* (México City: Ediciones ERA, 1969); p. 22: Carlos Monsiváis, in *Siempre!* (April 1968); pp. 49, 51: Geir Kjetsaa, *Fyodor Dostoyevsky: A Writer's Life* (New York: Random House, Inc., 1987); p. 55: Nancy Newhall, ed., *The Daybooks of Edward Weston* (New York: Aperture, 1990); p. 106: Elena Poniatowska, *Fuerte es el silencio* (México City: Ediciones ERA, 1980); p. 134: Yevgeny Yevtushenko, Forward to *The Russian Century*, by Brian Moynahan (New York: Random House, Inc., 1994).

Library of Congress Catalog Card Number: 97-75183
Hardcover ISBN: 0-89381-776-7

Printed and bound by Everbest Printing Company Ltd., Hong Kong

Book and jacket design by Wendy Byrne

The Staff at Aperture for *Juárez: The Laboratory of Our Future* is:
Michael E. Hoffman, *Executive Director*
Melissa Harris, *Editor*
Stevan A. Baron, *Production Director*
Elizabeth Franzen, *Managing Editor*
Lesley A. Martin, *Assistant Editor*
Nell Elizabeth Farrell, Maura Shea, *Editorial Assistants*
Helen Marra, *Production Manager*
David Frankel, *Copy Editor*
Cara Maniaci, *Editorial Work-Scholar*
Serena Park, *Production Work-Scholar*

Thanks to Carlos Vigueras of Casa de las Americas for coordinating photographs and captions on behalf of many of the photographers.

Some captions translated from the original Spanish by Cola Franzen.

A traveling exhibition based on *Juárez: The Laboratory of Our Future*, organized by DiverseWorks in Houston in collaboration with Aperture and in conjunction with FotoFest 1998, is available through Aperture. Please contact Launa Beuhler at (212) 505-5555, ext. 327.

Aperture Foundation publishes a periodical, books, and portfolios of fine photography to communicate with serious photographers and creative people everywhere. A complete catalog is available upon request.
Address: 20 East 23rd Street, New York, New York 10010.
Phone: (212) 598-4205. Fax: (212) 598-4015.
Toll-free: (800) 929-2323.

Aperture Foundation books are distributed internationally through:
CANADA: General Publishing, 30 Lesmill Road, Don Mills, Ontario, M3B 2T6. Fax: (416) 445-5991. UNITED KINGDOM, SCANDANAVIA AND CONTINENTAL EUROPE: Robert Hale, Ltd., Clerkenwell House, 45-47 Clerkenwell Green, London EC1R OHT. Fax: 171-490-4958. NETHERLANDS: Nilsson & Lamm, BV, Pampuslaan 212-214, P.O. Box 195, 1382 JS Weesp, Netherlands. Fax: 31-294-415054.

For international magazine subscription orders for the periodical *Aperture*, contact Aperture International Subscription Service, P.O. Box 14, Harold Hill, Romford, RM3 8EQ, England. Fax: 1-708-372-046. One year: £30.00. Price subject to change.

To subscribe to the periodical *Aperture* in the U.S.A. write Aperture, P.O. Box 3000, Denville, NJ 07834.
Phone: 1-800-783-4903. One year: $40.00.

First edition
10 9 8 7 6 5 4 3 2 1